Insights for Becoming an Effective Leader

LEADERSHIP LESSONS FROM THE BIBLE.

For I can do everything through Jesus Christ, who gives me strength.
- Philippians 4:13

Pradeep Kasab

BLUEROSE PUBLISHERS
India | U.K.

Copyright © Pradeep Kasab 2023

All rights reserved by author. No part of this publication may be reproduced, stored in a retrieval system or transmitted in any form or by any means, electronic, mechanical, photocopying, recording or otherwise, without the prior permission of the author. Although every precaution has been taken to verify the accuracy of the information contained herein, the publisher assumes no responsibility for any errors or omissions. No liability is assumed for damages that may result from the use of information contained within.

BlueRose Publishers takes no responsibility for any damages, losses, or liabilities that may arise from the use or misuse of the information, products, or services provided in this publication.

For permissions requests or inquiries regarding this publication, please contact:

BLUEROSE PUBLISHERS
www.BlueRoseONE.com
info@bluerosepublishers.com
+91 8882 898 898
+4407342408967

ISBN: 978-93-5989-043-2

Cover design: Muskan Sachdeva
Typesetting: Rohit

First Edition: November 2023

"Leadership Lessons from the Bible: Insights for Becoming an Effective Leader" is intended solely for the purpose of providing leadership insights and guidance based on stories and lessons from the Bible. This book does not intend to harm, cast judgment, or promote any particular religious denomination or beliefs. The author's objective is to draw inspiration from biblical narratives and offer universal leadership principles that can be applied by individuals from diverse backgrounds and belief systems.

Readers are encouraged to approach the content with an open mind, respecting their own faith and understanding that the book's focus is on leadership development, not religious doctrine. The author acknowledges the rich tapestry of religious beliefs and encourages all readers to interpret the lessons in a manner that aligns with their personal values and convictions.

It is important to remember that the interpretations and applications of biblical stories may vary among individuals. The author's intent is to inspire and educate, without any intention to challenge or undermine any religious beliefs. We hope that readers of all faiths and backgrounds will find value in the leadership insights shared within these pages.

By reading this book, you acknowledge and accept the intent of the author and Publisher

Book Introduction:

"Leadership Lessons from the Bible: Insights for Becoming an Effective Leader" delves into the rich tapestry of biblical events and people to glean important lessons for leadership in the contemporary world. The Bible, with its many different storylines, has a wealth of wisdom that is not limited by the confines of time, society, or religion. In this book, we dig into fifteen riveting chapters that reveal profound insights and principles that may guide and inspire individuals on their road towards being successful leaders. These insights and principles can help individuals on their journey towards becoming more effective leaders.

Each chapter focuses on a particular biblical tale and its protagonist, illuminating their excellent leadership traits and the lessons that may be gained from their experiences. These stories are from the Old and New Testaments. Regardless of our professional or religious origins, these age-old stories can teach us lessons that are both applicable and instructive in the modern world. By delving into the lives of powerful people in the Bible, we can get a more profound comprehension of the underlying principles that govern good leadership.

This book is filled with stories of outstanding leaders who overcame tremendous obstacles, handled challenging decisions, and demonstrated remarkable character characteristics. Each chapter presents a novel viewpoint on the topic of leadership and provides the reader with important lessons to glean from the material presented. These viewpoints range from the integrity of Joseph to the strategic thinking of David, from the bravery of Moses to the wisdom of King Solomon.

We learn the value of teamwork, inspiration, resiliency, loyalty, and diplomacy in leadership by analysing the leadership styles and methods of biblical personalities such as Nehemiah, Deborah, Daniel, Ruth, Joshua, and Esther. These biblical people all played significant roles in the Bible. In addition, we investigate the life-changing experiences of Paul and Peter, and we bear testimony to their maturation, tenacity, and capacity to gain wisdom from their past errors.

In addition, we glean lessons on prudence, wisdom, and the art of making sound decisions by drawing on the counsel contained in the book of Proverbs. We investigate the servant leadership of Jesus, who modelled characteristics like humility, selflessness, and compassion. His example has left an indelible effect on history and has served as an inspiration to numerous leaders over the years.

In the end, we investigate the peaceful teamwork that existed among the apostles and investigate how they constructed a powerful leadership team that was responsible for laying the groundwork for early Christian society.

The readers of "Leadership Lessons from the Bible: Insights for Becoming an Effective Leader" will start on a transforming journey towards developing and strengthening their leadership abilities because of the compelling anecdotes, practical insights, and thought-provoking reflections that are contained within the pages of the book. This book will equip you with timeless knowledge and practical tactics for becoming a successful and influential leader. Whether you are an experienced leader searching for new views or an aspiring leader looking for direction, this book will provide you with the tools you need.

Contents:

1. The Wisdom of Solomon: Leading with Discernment 1
2. Moses and the Exodus: Visionary Leadership in Times of Crisis 7
3. David and Goliath: Courage and Strategic Thinking 13
4. Joseph's Journey: Integrity and Resilience in Leadership 19
5. Nehemiah and Rebuilding the Wall: Mobilizing and Inspiring a Team 26
6. Deborah and Barak: Collaboration and Empowering Others 33
7. Daniel's Exemplary Character: Leading with Integrity in a Hostile Environment 39
8. Ruth's Loyalty and Servant Leadership 46
9. Joshua and the Battle of Jericho: Leading with Boldness and Faith 52
10. Esther's Influence: Leadership through Diplomacy and Risk-taking 58
11. Paul's Transformation: From Persecutor to Apostle of the Early Church 64
12. Peter's Leadership in the Early Christian Community: Learning from Mistakes 70
13. Prudence and Wisdom: Lessons from Proverbs for Effective Leadership 76

14. Jesus as the Ultimate Leader: Humility and Sacrifice.. 82
15. The Apostles' Unity and Collaboration: Building a Strong Leadership Team 88
End Note: 109

Chapter 1:

The Wisdom of Solomon: Leading with Discernment

There aren't many historical characters that can compare to King Solomon in terms of their reputation for being wise. Solomon's leadership is renowned for its extraordinary discernment and impeccable judgement, and it provides lessons that are useful for aspiring leaders in any period.

Solomon succeeded his father, King David, on the throne of Israel and inherited a country that was flourishing and prosperous throughout his father's reign. On the other hand, he was well aware of the significance of preserving and expanding upon the accomplishments of his father. Solomon was aware of the requirement of seeking the guidance of the divine and making prudent choices to exercise discernment in his leadership.

The story of the two women who claimed to be the mother of a newborn infant is one of the most well-known examples of Solomon's wisdom, and it is also one of the most renowned anecdotes. Solomon came up with an original idea for a resolution when both of the ladies brought their issues to his attention. He proposed severing the infant in two, with each mother getting an equal portion of the resulting halves. The child's real mother, who was overflowing with love and compassion, made an instant offer to renounce her parental rights to save her child's life. Solomon, seeing the true mother's devotion, gave her custody of the kid after deciding that she should be the primary carer. This episode demonstrated Solomon's capacity to recognise lies and arrive at just conclusions, even when faced with challenging circumstances that were fraught with intense emotion.

Solomon's wisdom expanded beyond specific circumstances to include government on a more systemic level. He instituted new laws and regulations that helped advance the cause of justice and fairness. His famous ruling in the argument between two ladies over who should have custody of a baby is one example of this type of situation. Solomon exercised his wisdom to determine who the biological mother of the kid was by posing a question about the health of the child as a test. Because of his keen ability to distinguish the genuine from the fraudulent, justice was able to triumph across his dominion.

In addition, Solomon's knowledge extended beyond the realm of law to include administration, diplomacy, and strategic decision-making. He was a master in all these areas. He used foresight by establishing alliances through marriage contracts, which resulted in peace and stability for his kingdom because of his actions. Because of his foresight in managing tricky diplomatic issues, he was able to have amicable ties with the countries that bordered his realm, which in turn further bolstered the realm's security and prosperity.

Solomon's wisdom did not originate merely from his exceptional intelligence; rather, it sprang from the profound veneration with which he held God. Recognising that genuine knowledge must originate from above, he prayed for heavenly direction and continued to abide by the laws that God had established. The realisation that his position as a leader was a stewardship that had been bestowed on him was what enabled him to lead with humility and discernment. He relied on a higher power to do this.

From Solomon's example as a leader, aspiring leaders may learn numerous essential lessons. To begin, developing discernment takes making a conscious effort to increase one's levels of knowledge, comprehension, and insight. To make decisions that are in line with the best interests of the organisation, leaders need to demonstrate a commitment to ongoing learning and growth. Second, successful leaders need to be able to go behind the surface of difficult circumstances and unearth the facts that lie underneath the surface. A sharp eye for specifics, attentive hearing, and careful observation are all necessary components of the discernment process.

In addition, those in positions of authority should make efforts towards fairness and justice, considering the requirements and considerations of all parties involved. Solomon's judgements served as illustrative examples of his dedication to maintaining righteousness and ensuring that justice predominated throughout his reign. In conclusion, humility, and acknowledgement of one's own need for a higher force should be at the foundation of a leader's wisdom. The ability to lead with discernment requires actively seeking direction, maintaining a teachable mindset, and being honest about one's limits.

Key Take Aways:

As a leader, exercising discernment is a strategy that entails making judgements that are intelligent and well-informed, considering all of the information that is available, and allowing your judgement to guide your actions. The following is a list of important beliefs and practises that can help you lead with discernment:

Collect Information to ensure that the choices you make are well-informed, it is important to collect as much pertinent information as you can. This may require carrying out research, requesting advice from members of the team as well as specialists, and keeping up to speed with the latest developments in the business.

Active listening is giving full attention to the people around you, including coworkers, superiors, and subordinates. Listen carefully to the comments, suggestions, and worries that they have. This not only enables you to make better judgements, but it also helps to create trust and foster a climate that is more conducive to collaboration.

Analyse properly Once you obtain the information you need, it is important to take the time to properly evaluate the material. Think about the many outcomes that may result from the various options you have, as well as the effects that your choices will have in the long run.

Your intuition is just as important as all the facts and analysis you've been poring over, so don't discount it. In many cases, trusting your instincts may give you with helpful information. It is the end consequence of the processing of knowledge and experience that occurs in your subconscious.

Considerations of Ethical Importance are Given Priority in Decision-Making Discerning leaders place a high value on the ethical implications of their choices. Think about the moral and ethical repercussions of your decisions and check to see that they are in line with the core values and guiding principles of your organisation.

Think About Stakeholders Recognise the influence that your actions will have on a variety of stakeholders, including as workers, customers, shareholders, and the community at large. Make it a priority to arrive at decisions that consider the needs and concerns of all involved parties.

Seek Out Diverse Points of View Seek out and encourage a variety of points of view and views from inside your team. Different angles of view can aid in the detection of blind spots and lead to judgements that are more balanced overall.

Being decisive means that, while giving anything significant thought is vital, it is equally crucial to make judgements in a timely manner. Avoid being stuck in analysis paralysis by making it a goal to establish a balance between being thorough and meeting deadlines.

Capacity for Adaptation: Recognise that the outcomes of your actions won't always be what you anticipate. A perceptive leader maintains their ability to adapt and is willing to modify their strategy if fresh knowledge or shifting circumstances necessitate it.

Communication ensure that you effectively explain your decisions to your team, as well as the reasoning that went into making those decisions. Increasing both trust and comprehension requires not only openness but also effective communication.

Reflecting on your own actions and the results of those actions on a regular basis is an important part of the self-reflection process. You may continuously develop your capacity to lead with discernment by taking the lessons you can learn from both your triumphs and your mistakes.

Set a positive example for your team by acting as a model of discernment and sound judgement. The culture of your organisation will be shaped by both the decisions you make and the activities you do.

To lead with discernment, you need to strike a balance between logical analysis and intuitive understanding. It requires taking into consideration the larger context, as well as ethical concerns and the requirements of a variety of stakeholders. You will be able to make decisions that are better informed and more deliberate if you put these principles into practise, decisions that will contribute to the success and integrity of your organisation.

Chapter 2:

Moses and the Exodus: Visionary Leadership in Times of Crisis

The narrative of Moses and the Israelites' departure from Egypt serves as a remarkable illustration of faith, tenacity, and visionary leadership in the face of overwhelming hardship. Moses displays the attributes of a leader who can steer a group through difficult times and direct it towards a brighter future. Moses was selected by God to free the Israelites from slavery, and he did so by demonstrating these abilities.

The beginning of Moses' path as a leader began with a calling from God. Amid the forest, while he was tending to his flock, he came upon a bush that was ablaze but had not been burned by the fire. During this miraculous meeting, God revealed His plan to liberate the Israelites from their slavery in Egypt and designated Moses as their leader. God also gave Moses the Ten Commandments to teach the Israelites. Moses, despite his initial hesitation and self-doubt, accepted the challenge and set out on a path towards becoming a more transformative leader.

Moses' confrontation with Pharaoh, the ruler of Egypt, was a shining example of visionary leadership on his part. He had a crystal-clear vision of independence and emancipation for his people, and he fought relentlessly for the rights of his people. Pharaoh was faced by Moses, who showed unyielding commitment, and Moses pleaded with Pharaoh to let the Israelites go free so that they might worship their God in the desert. His vision acted as a compass for the Israelites, pointing them in the right direction and giving them reason to have hope and perseverance despite the challenges they faced.

Throughout the Exodus, Moses was put through several ordeals and examinations of his leadership. Even though he had to negotiate with Pharaoh and observe the plagues that befell Egypt, he did not waiver in his determination. Moses had an extraordinary amount of confidence and trust in God when the Israelites were cornered between the Red Sea and the Egyptian army that was pursuing them. The Israelites were able to cross the sea to safety because of a miraculous parting of the waters brought about by divine intervention. Even amid the most difficult of circumstances, Moses' constant faith in God's power and supply proved the visionary leadership that he possessed.

In addition to this, Moses was a remarkable leader in that he was able to adjust to changing circumstances. It was not an easy assignment to oversee guiding a huge group through the tough circumstances of the wilderness. Moses stayed dedicated to his goal and continued to lead his people forward while suffering opposition from his people in the form of complaints, internal strife, and periods of uncertainty. He guided the Israelites through difficult situations, such as a lack of food and water, and provided remedies while also working to promote unity among them. As an example of the significance of adaptability and resilience in visionary leadership, consider Moses. He was able to adjust to ever-changing conditions while still maintaining his position as leader.

In addition to this, Moses' leadership went beyond simply directing the Israelites in a physical sense. In addition to this, by the revelation of the commandments of God, he gave them a framework for morality and ethics. Moses, in his role as an intermediary between God and the people, forged a covenant that obligated the Israelites to conduct their lives following the laws that God had created. The importance of ethical leadership, as well as the obligation of leaders to set a good example for their followers, is highlighted by his function as both a moral guide and an arbitrator of justice.

The narrative of Moses and the Exodus has a lot to teach leaders about how to handle difficult situations when they arise. During times of upheaval, it is helpful to have leaders who possess the kind of visionary leadership that is characterised by a compelling and crystal-clear vision. The leaders of a group need to be able to explain a vision that fires up their members gives them reason to have hope and gets them motivated to take action.

Both resilience and adaptability are necessary for leaders, as they must be able to persevere in the face of adversity and maintain their focus throughout the process. The value of resilience in leadership is highlighted by the fact that Moses was able to persevere through challenges, keep his attention on the task at hand, and come up with inventive solutions.

In addition, the importance of ethical leadership which is founded on moral ideals and a dedication to justice cannot be overstated. Not only should leaders move their communities ahead, but they should also serve as a moral compass that directs the conduct of their followers and encourages a feeling of togetherness and common purpose.

Key Take Aways:

In times of crisis, visionary leadership is an essential technique that entails motivating individuals and organisations to persevere through difficult and unpredictable circumstances by providing direction and inspiration. A visionary leader not only solves the pressing problems at hand but also looks beyond the current predicament and imagines a more favourable future. In challenging times, visionary leadership requires adhering to several fundamental principles and best practises, which are as follows:

Keep Your Vision in Focus A visionary leader is one who, even in the middle of a crisis, can maintain a vision for the future that is both crystal clear and captivating. This vision ought to offer hope and direction, acting as a guiding light for the organisation and the individuals that make up its membership.

Communicate in an Efficient Manner Open and consistent communication is of the utmost importance. Maintain communication with your team on the present situation, the actions being taken, and the long-term goals. Communication that is both open and honest helps to create trust and decreases uncertainty.

Empower your team to take ownership of their jobs and encourage them to work towards the common vision. Empower your team to take responsibility of their roles and inspire them to work towards the common vision. To discover answers to the issue, ingenuity and creativity should be encouraged.

Set a good example by ensuring that your behaviours are consistent with the goals you have set for yourself. Show that you can bounce back from adversity, adapt, and have a positive mindset. Your actions will serve as a model for the rest of your team.

Encourage a spirit of oneness and cooperation via the process of collaboration. It is important to foster a culture of cooperation not just within your organisation but also with external partners. During a time of crisis, collaboration can lead to the development of more efficient solutions.

Ability to adapt: Maintain an open mind and modify your behaviour in response to changing conditions. To successfully navigate the unpredictability of a crisis, flexibility is very necessary.

Thinking strategically entails keeping an eye on the bigger picture while tackling pressing issues in the here and now. Take into consideration how the crisis may affect your sector as well as any chances that may arise as a result.

Embrace innovation: During times of crisis, people frequently come up with fresh ideas and approaches to problem solving. Your staff should be encouraged and supported in coming up with inventive solutions to problems.

Readiness in a Crisis Learn from the present crisis and utilise the experience to strengthen the crisis readiness of your organisation for the future by learning from the current crisis.

Maintain your own level of resilience and urge the other members of your team to do the same. You can quickly recover from failures and continue to make progress towards your goals when you have resilience.

Evaluation and cautious administration of hazards are required for effective risk management. A visionary leader is someone who understands the possible risks and uncertainties, as well as the ability to devise solutions to reduce such risks and uncertainties.

Recognise the emotional toll that a crisis may take on the individuals of your team and show empathy for them. Exhibit empathy, provide support, and make resources available for the mental and emotional well of others.

Establishing Clear, quantifiable Goals and Milestones It is important to establish clear, quantifiable goals and milestones to measure progress towards the vision. Maintain a consistent evaluation process and adapt your methods as necessary.

Take Advantage of the Crisis as a Learning Opportunity Take advantage of the situation as a learning and development opportunity. Think about what went well and what didn't, and then try to incorporate these learnings into your future endeavours.

Instilling optimism and a sense of direction during a crisis is a necessary component of providing visionary leadership, even if the future is unclear. It entails motivating your team to triumph over obstacles, adjust to new circumstances, and eventually emerge in a better position. You will be able to assist your organisation in navigating crises with resilience and purpose if you keep a clear vision and adhere to these principles.

Chapter 3:

David and Goliath: Courage and Strategic Thinking

The ageless story of David and Goliath has been captivating audiences for generations, demonstrating the extraordinary power of bravery and smart thought in the face of obstacles that appear to be insurmountable. David, a young boy who worked as a shepherd, exemplifies the idea that genuine leadership does not depend on one's physical size but rather on one's moral fortitude and one's capacity to plan and make decisions intelligently.

Fear filled the hearts of even the most experienced Israelites fighters as they met the Philistine giant Goliath, who stood over nine feet tall and was armed with fearsome armour and weaponry. Goliath was a member of the Philistine race. David, on the other hand, despite having nothing more than a simple shepherd's sling and an unshakable faith, volunteered to go up against the intimidating Goliath. In the face of challenges, his bravery and resolve shone as an illuminating illustration of effective leadership.

David's demonstration of bravery always stemmed from his unshakable conviction in God's might and his steadfast faith in God's providential care for him. He refused to be persuaded by the uncertainties and anxieties of those around him, opting instead to put his confidence in the direction and safety that God would provide. David's courage in facing Goliath came from his firm belief that the struggle did not belong to him alone but rather to the Lord, and that he was only acting as the Lord's agent. The Israelite army gained a newfound feeling of optimism and resolve as a direct result of his bravery, which served as an inspiration to others.

However, David's leadership was not entirely dependent on the bravery he showed on his own. He distinguished himself from his competitors using strategic thinking. David devised a crafty plan since he was aware of the inherent disadvantages of facing Goliath in close-quarters warfare. David's ability with the sling allowed him to hit the monster from a distance rather than engage in a confrontation with Goliath on his terms. David skilfully targeted Goliath's weak spot, the forehead, and killed his adversary with a single stone to the head by taking advantage of Goliath's frailty.

Beyond the confines of the battlefield, David's strategic thinking extended. As a leader, he was aware of the need to be well-prepared and make the most of available possibilities. David refined his abilities as a shepherd by defending his sheep from various wild beasts in the years leading up to their confrontation with Goliath. This experience provided him with the dexterity, accuracy, and strategic attitude that were essential for him to take on Goliath. David's leadership was a shining example of the need to make full use of one's unique set of abilities, experiences, and perspectives to triumph over difficult obstacles.

In addition, David's humility and a strong sense of purpose complemented both his bravery and his ability to think strategically. David didn't let his win over Goliath make him arrogant, and he didn't take advantage of his newfound popularity either. Instead, he remained King Saul's steadfast and trustworthy counsel throughout their whole relationship. The example of David's humble leadership demonstrates how important it is to put one's position and influence to work for the benefit of others rather than for one's gain.

The battle between David and Goliath has many valuable lessons for leaders in today's world. To begin, it serves as a timely reminder that bravery is not the absence of fear but rather the capacity to triumph over it. True leaders can admit their anxieties without allowing those fears to paralyse them. They derive courage from their beliefs, keep their composure in the face of opposition, and motivate others around them via the unyielding resolve with which they pursue their goals.

Two, being able to think strategically is a prerequisite for becoming a leader. To effectively confront issues, leaders are required to analyse circumstances, determine their strengths and limitations, and devise novel solutions. They, like David, will need to be flexible and willing to think creatively to attain their goals, making the most of the specific abilities and resources at their disposal.

In conclusion, humility is a quality that distinguishes great leaders from average ones. Humble leaders place a higher value on the well-being of the group than on their accolades. They foster devotion and confidence, producing an atmosphere in which collaboration and expansion may flourish.

Key Take Aways:

It takes both bravery and the ability to think strategically in order to be an effective leader and to make decisions that are in the best interests of the organisation. The following exemplifies how well they go together:

Goal setting with a Strategic Attitude Strategic thinking frequently entails goal-setting with a strategic attitude and the pursuit of new possibilities. It takes bravery to put oneself in harm's way and follow one's ambitions when one does not know how things will turn out. A daring leader is one who is ready to push themselves beyond their comfort zone to accomplish their strategic goals.

Taking Difficult Decisions: Thinking strategically necessitates taking difficult decisions, such as reallocating resources, expanding into new markets, or reorganising the organisation. It requires bravery to make these decisions, particularly when they involve substantial change and the possibility of backlash from several parties.

Conquering Opposition: In the process of putting a strategy plan into action, executives may come up against opposition from workers, customers, or other stakeholders. To face this opposition head-on, listen to concerns, and articulate the benefits of the strategic direction requires a lot of courage.

Both innovation and adaptability are essential components of strategic thinking, which entails looking for novel approaches to problems and adjusting to ever-evolving environments. To maintain their position as competitive and relevant, courageous leaders are prepared to challenge the status quo and are receptive to new ideas.

Assuming Responsibility Bold leaders accept full responsibility for the results of their strategic choices, regardless of whether those choices were successful. They are not afraid to accept responsibility for their actions, and they are eager to grow from their mistakes and adapt their plans accordingly.

Communication: Being able to communicate effectively is essential for both courageous thinking and strategic thinking. To inspire and motivate their teams, leaders need to express their strategic vision in a way that is both clear and convincing.

By setting an example for their teams and exhibiting a willingness to accept strategic change and take calculated risks, courageous leaders teach their followers the value of leading by example. This motivates other people to follow in your footsteps.

Getting Over Your Fear of Failing Fear of failing may be a big obstacle to strategic thinking and must be managed. The ability to face their fears and go forth with confidence, even though making strategic decisions inevitably involves some level of risk, is made possible by the trait of courage.

Strategic thinking frequently requires adopting a long-term view to be effective. When faced with short-term problems or defeats, courageous leaders can maintain their dedication to the strategic direction of the organisation.

Resilience: Leaders who can combine bravery with strategic thinking have a higher level of resilience when confronted with adversity. They can recover quickly from defeats and reversals while keeping their focus on the long-term goals they have set for themselves.

Ethical Considerations Brave leaders are unafraid to make judgements that are ethical, even though doing so may be difficult. Thinking strategically requires taking into consideration the moral and ethical repercussions of actions and having the fortitude to act morally even when doing so presents challenges.

In conclusion, bravery, and the ability to think strategically are two complementing qualities that help leaders to establish audacious goals, come to difficult judgements, and successfully traverse the intricacies of a corporate environment that is always shifting. When brought together in an efficient manner, they have the potential to provide innovative and successful leadership that propels an organisation towards achieving its strategic goals.

Chapter 4:

Joseph's Journey: Integrity and Resilience in Leadership

The incredible journey that Joseph took from being a favoured son to becoming a great leader in Egypt serves as a stunning tribute to the traits of integrity and resilience that are essential in a leader. The transforming impact of preserving one's integrity and the ability to bounce back from trying circumstances is demonstrated by Joseph's unshakable devotion to doing what is right, even in the face of hardship.

The narrative of Joseph begins with his father Jacob favouring Joseph above his siblings, which ultimately leads to jealousy and treachery on the part of Joseph's brothers. Joseph had several hardships during his life, one of which was being sold into slavery by his siblings. Nevertheless, despite the wrongs that he was subjected to, he never wavered in his dedication to upholding integrity and doing what is right.

Joseph, while serving as a slave in the household of Potiphar, was known for his amazing honesty and attention to his task. Because he had proven himself worthy of his master's confidence, the latter appointed him to a position of power inside the family. Joseph rebuffed his master's wife's attempts because he was aware of the ethical and legal repercussions that would result from breaking the confidence of his master. Potiphar's wife sought to seduce Joseph. To demonstrate the significance of sustaining ethical standards in leadership, one need only look at Joseph's unshakeable integrity and his reluctance to compromise his values.

When Joseph was falsely accused of attempted rape and imprisoned, his perseverance was put to the test in a new and more difficult way. Despite the challenges he faced, he continued to exhibit resiliency and an optimistic attitude. Even within the confines of the black jail walls, his honesty showed through. Because Joseph was able to keep his cool, provide advice, and interpret Pharaoh's dreams, he was eventually released from prison and elevated to a position of significant influence in Pharaoh's court.

Despite the challenges he faced as Egypt's leader, Joseph was able to maintain his composure and remain flexible. When a severe famine ravaged the region, Joseph created a scheme to stockpile food during years of abundance. By doing this, he ensured the survival of both the Egyptian people and the populations of the nations who were neighbouring Egypt. The value of tenacity and insight cannot be overstated when it comes to navigating stormy times. His leadership is visionary, and he can predict and prepare for future obstacles.

In addition, Joseph's journey imparts wisdom to us on the power of reconciliation and forgiveness. Joseph was presented with the opportunity to exact his revenge on his brothers when, during the famine, they returned to Egypt pleading for aid in their search for food. Instead, he chose to forgive them and let them into his life, which ultimately led to reconciliation and healing within his family. The example that Joseph sets is a potent reminder that leaders who possess integrity are not motivated by revenge but rather by a desire for unity and restoration, and this lesson may be learned from Joseph's life.

The account of Joseph's journey has many valuable lessons that apply to leaders in today's world. To begin, having integrity is necessary to be an effective leader. Even in the face of temptation or challenge, those in leadership positions are expected to prioritise ethical behaviour. Maintaining one's integrity not only wins one the trust and respect of one's peers, but it also lays a solid groundwork for one's ability to achieve success in the long run.

Second, for leaders to be successful in overcoming challenges and emerging even more powerful, resilience is an absolute must. The fact that Joseph was able to overcome obstacles such as treachery, false charges, and incarceration exemplifies the significance of maintaining a good attitude and tenacity. Adversity should be seen as an opportunity for personal and professional progress, and leaders should take advantage of these learning and growth possibilities presented by setbacks.

Finally, leaders have access to strong instruments that may help them establish bridges and nurture unity: forgiveness and reconciliation. Not only did Joseph's act of forgiveness towards his brothers rebuild connections with them, but it also created the conditions for the group to heal and mature. Leaders who can extend forgiveness and seek reconciliation are in a better position to establish a climate that fosters cooperation, trust, and creativity.

Key Take Aways:

Integrity and resilience are two essential attributes that are essential to good leadership and play a significant part in the function. They are complementing characteristics that contribute to a leader's capacity to handle problems, inspire trust, and uphold ethical standards. Those are the three things that a good leader should be able to do. Integrity and resilience are crucial qualities in leaders for the following reasons:

Having integrity:

Integrity is the cornerstone of trustworthiness, which is why honesty is so important. Honesty, transparency, and consistency in both their words and deeds are hallmarks of leaders that possess integrity. They keep their word and do what they say they will, which helps build trust among the members of the team and the stakeholders.

Making Ethical judgements: Leaders with integrity can make ethical judgements, even when it's challenging to do so. They consider the ethical repercussions of their decisions while also placing the welfare of their team and the organisation above everything else.

Accountability: They are willing to accept blame for their behaviours and the choices they make. When errors occur, leaders with integrity own their responsibility, try to improve as a result of the blunders, and try to correct the situation.

Leaders are responsible for modelling appropriate behaviour for their teams. When leaders act with integrity, they inspire the members of their team to do the same, which contributes to the development of an environment that values honesty and ethical conduct.

Integrity relies heavily on a person's ability to maintain coherence between their words and deeds. It guarantees that the behaviour of the leader will continue to be trustworthy and predictable.

Resistance to harm:

Capacity for Adaptation: Resilient leaders can adjust in the face of change or difficulty. They look at difficulties as chances for personal development and education, and they urge the members of their team to be open to change as well.

Problem-Solving Resilience is defined as the ability to effectively solve problems and the capacity to discover answers regardless of how challenging the situation may be. Positive and solution-focused mindset is essential for a resilient leader to retain.

Emotional Intelligence: Resilient leaders have a high degree of emotional intelligence, which enables them to manage their own emotions and help their team members during times of difficulty.

Endurance: The ability to withstand negative experiences and carry on regardless of obstructions is an essential component of resilience. Leaders that exhibit resilience are not quickly discouraged and are able to motivate their followers to keep moving forwards even when things become difficult.

Self-Care Resilient leaders understand the significance of prioritising their own health and happiness. They prepare themselves both physically and mentally to meet the difficulties of leadership by taking the appropriate precautions.

Integrity and resiliency as essential components of effective leadership:

Ethical Resilience: Leaders who possess both integrity and resilience are better suited to deal with crises and challenging situations while upholding ethical standards since both traits are built to withstand adversity. They stay constant in their dedication to ethical behaviour, which allows them to make difficult decisions while maintaining their integrity.

Trust and Confidence: Having integrity helps to establish trust, while having confidence helps to build resilience. When members of a team have faith in their leader's honesty and ability to make ethical decisions, as well as when they observe their leader's capacity to persevere in the face of adversity, the team experiences a significant boost in its sense of security and confidence.

Management of Crises: In times of crisis, leaders who have integrity and resilience are well-equipped to lead their organisations through obstacles while preserving the trust of their stakeholders. This is essential to the success of crisis management. They make judgements in accordance with their principles and manage their team with resiliency and commitment.

Long-Term Success: Integrity and resiliency are two qualities that, when combined, contribute to the long-term success of an organisation. A leader who takes judgements that are compatible with ethical standards and who can adjust to changing circumstances with resilience is able to steer an organisation through a variety of obstacles while preserving its reputation and capacity to continue operating in the long term.

In a nutshell, the traits of honesty and resilience are necessary for leaders. Leaders that exhibit both characteristics inspire trust in their followers, make judgements that are morally sound, are flexible in the face of change, and are able to guide their teams through challenging situations with fortitude and resolve.

Chapter 5:

Nehemiah and Rebuilding the Wall: Mobilizing and Inspiring a Team

The tale of Nehemiah and the reconstruction of the wall of Jerusalem is a compelling illustration of the significance of motivating and encouraging a group of people to work together towards the accomplishment of a common objective. Nehemiah's leadership is illustrative of the attributes of vision, passion, and successful team management. It provides helpful insights into the art of rallying people together for a common purpose since it displays these qualities.

Nehemiah, who served as the cupbearer for the Persian monarch Artaxerxes, was given upsetting information regarding the condition of Jerusalem's walls. The city was in ruins, and its citizens were left defenceless and disheartened as a result. Nehemiah set out on a journey to restore the city's walls and revitalise the community. He was driven by a profound sense of purpose and an intense yearning to bring the city back to its former glory.

First and foremost, one of the most important aspects of Nehemiah's leadership was the crystal-clear vision he had and his unyielding dedication to the mission at hand. He inspired the people with a compelling picture of a city that had been fortified, which gave them hope and brought them together around a shared goal. The citizens of Jerusalem were profoundly moved by Nehemiah's vision of a rebuilt city, which sparked a sense of collective pride and unwavering determination among them.

Nehemiah was able to display outstanding competence around communication, which is necessary for mobilising and motivating a group of people. He addressed the people in a strategic manner, explaining the importance of their goal as well as its sense of urgency. Nehemiah was able to foster a feeling of unity and purpose in the community by the sharing of his personal connection to the city as well as his empathy for the challenges faced by the community. His ability to communicate in a way that was both clear and genuine was a significant factor in his success in gaining support and motivating others to act.

In addition, Nehemiah was aware of the necessity of incorporating the people in the process of rebuilding. He made sure that each individual and each group of individuals had a task that they were responsible for by delegating responsibilities and assigning particular obligations. The inclusive way Nehemiah led the people helped to cultivate a sense of ownership and empowerment among them, which in turn increased their level of commitment and dedication to the project. Nehemiah was able to bring out the full potential of his team by appreciating the efforts of each individual member and fostering an atmosphere that encouraged teamwork.

Nehemiah saw his fair share of challenges and criticism during the process of rebuilding the wall. As is the case with any endeavour, this is unavoidable. He shown an incredible amount of tenacity and unshakeable drive-in spite of the dangers that came from the outside as well as from within. The tenacity with which Nehemiah carried out his leadership responsibilities in the face of challenges was both an inspiration and a driver for his group. He led by example, exhibiting bravery and an unwillingness to be discouraged, which motivated the people to persist despite the challenging conditions they were facing.

Nehemiah was capable of not just galvanising and motivating the people, but also displaying excellent problem-solving talents. When confronted with opposition from adversaries in the surrounding area, he formulated tactical strategies to defend the workers and assure their safety. Because Nehemiah was able to evaluate potential threats, formulate responses, and remain flexible in the face of shifting conditions, the work of rebuilding was able to go without interruption. The success of the team's goals can be directly attributed to his leadership, which shows the significance of strategic thinking and proactive problem-solving.

The tale of Nehemiah and the reconstruction of the wall of Jerusalem has several valuable lessons that may be applied in modern leadership. To inspire and motivate a group of people, it is essential to have a well-defined vision and to successfully communicate that vision to them. Leaders have an obligation to include and empower the members of their teams, as well as to recognise and appreciate the contributions of those individuals and to create an atmosphere that encourages collaboration. In addition to this, leaders should be able to show that they are resilient in the face of adversity and possess the ability to solve problems to prevail over hurdles along the road.

Key Take Aways:

One of the most important aspects of good leadership is the ability to motivate and encourage one's team. When a leader can excite their team, direct their efforts towards a common purpose, and drive them towards shared goals, the team as a whole is able to achieve greater levels of success, engagement, and productivity. The following are some effective methods for motivating and inspiring a team:

Establish a Crystal-Clear Vision and Goal:

Establish a compelling vision for the team that describes the path to take and the objectives to achieve.

It is important to communicate the purpose of the team as well as how that goal fits into the overall mission of the organisation.

Assist individual team members in comprehending the significance of their efforts and the influence that their work has had.

Setting a Good Example:

Set an example for your team by exhibiting the beliefs, work ethic, and behaviours that you demand from them.

Demonstrate a commitment to the objectives of the team and take an active role in achieving those objectives.

Your deeds serve as an example for the rest of the team, motivating others to replicate what you've done.

Communication That Is Effective:

Encourage communication that is both open and honest among the members of the team.

Maintain an attentive listening posture towards the issues, suggestions, and comments raised by team members.

Expectations should be articulated clearly, regular updates should be provided, and any questions or concerns should be addressed.

Empower the People, then Delegate:

Make the members of the team responsible for their own decisions and delegate decision-making authority to them.

You should have faith in your team's ability to take responsibility for their job and make contributions that really matter.

Give them the freedom to develop and find their own solutions to challenges.

Acknowledge and consider:

Acknowledge and appreciate the accomplishments of both individuals and teams.

Acknowledge the effort that each member of the team has put in and thank them for their commitment.

A boost in morale and drive can be achieved through recognition.

Give Support and Make Resources Available:

Make it a priority to equip your team with the experience, tools, and materials it needs to be successful.

Make yourself available to them whenever they face difficulties or want direction.

Your team will have an easier time remaining engaged and motivated when roadblocks are removed.

Motivate with a Captivating Narrative:

Discuss anecdotes, personal experiences, and other examples that highlight the team's mission and objectives.

Create a clear image of the future that you want and the positive influence that the work of the team will have.

Stories are extremely effective methods for generating ideas.

Foster Personal Development and Academic Achievement:

Foster an environment that values lifelong education and constant progress.

Help out team members who are working on their professional growth and improving their skills.

Demonstrate that you are invested in their development in some way.

Create an Atmosphere That Is Uplifting and Accepting:

Develop a culture at your place of employment that recognises the significance of diversity, inclusiveness, and teamwork.

Take immediate action to resolve disagreements and problems if you want to keep the atmosphere at your place of employment cordial.

Foster collaboration and support for one another.

Give the Feeling of Being in Control:

Give each member of the team some latitude to make their own decisions within the scope of their task.

Encourage them to own their work and accept responsibility for the duties they are assigned.

The freedom to make one's own decisions boosts both motivation and inventiveness.

Adjust Yourself to the New:

Embrace change because it presents a chance for personal development and advancement.

Maintain a constructive and flexible attitude while guiding the team through the transitions.

Encourage everyone on the team to be adaptable and willing to accept change.

Continue to be Dedicated and Persistent:

Even in the face of difficulties, you should not waver in your commitment to the objectives and vision of the team.

Exhibit the sort of resiliency and commitment that may motivate your staff to achieve the same for themselves.

It is possible for leaders to successfully mobilise and inspire their teams by putting these ideas into action, therefore establishing a working environment that encourages motivation, productivity, and a feeling of shared purpose.

Chapter 6:

Deborah and Barak: Collaboration and Empowering Others

The narrative of Deborah and Barak, which can be found in the book of Judges, serves as a fascinating illustration of the power that may be harnessed via teamwork and giving others leadership roles. Deborah, a prophetess and judge of Israel, and Barak, a military leader, join forces to free their people from the oppression of their adversaries and save the day for Israel. Their cooperation exemplifies the significance of working together, taking turns in leadership roles, and delegating authority to others to achieve group goals.

Wisdom, insight, and a close relationship with God were hallmarks of Deborah's leadership, which she exhibited throughout the events she oversaw. She presided as a judge over the Israelites, mediating disagreements and advising them on proper conduct. When the people were threatened by the Canaanite army commanded by Sisera, Deborah sent for Barak and conveyed a word from God telling him to collect an army and attack those who were oppressing them. Barak did as God instructed and defeated the Canaanite army led by Sisera.

In the beginning, Barak was hesitant and voiced uncertainty that he could lead the charge. Because he recognised Deborah's exceptional wisdom and her close relationship to God, he asked Deborah to fight beside him in the war. Deborah gave her consent to accompany Barak, but she also made a prophecy that the glory of the triumph would be awarded to a woman and not to Barak. Her reaction indicated a readiness to appreciate the skills and capabilities of others around her as well as to give them the ability to empower themselves.

Collaboration between Deborah and Barak, as well as shared leadership, was essential to their accomplishments. They pooled their resources and consulted one another to devise an effective strategy and plan for the upcoming conflict. Deborah was the one who supplied direction and heavenly vision while Barak was the one who led the army into battle. Their collaboration produced a potent synergy that boosted morale and cohesion among the Israelite soldiers, and it was largely responsible for their victory.

Deborah's example of leadership that inspires confidence in others is one of the most impressive components of this narrative. She saw Barak's potential as a leader and urged him to take on the responsibilities that came with that position. Deborah decided not to take all of the credit for the triumph, but rather to empower Barak and give him the opportunity to realise his full potential. Not only did her act of empowering others raise Barak's status, but it also produced a sense of shared ownership and pride among the Israelites, which fuelled their drive to triumph over their oppressors.

In addition, Deborah's humility and open-mindedness were on full display when she was eager to cooperate with others and listen to the points of view of those around her.

She valued the comments and insights offered by Barak and the other leaders, and she encouraged their participation. The team was able to make well-informed decisions and perform to the best of their combined ability because of Deborah's inclusive leadership style, which created an atmosphere in which varied points of view were acknowledged.

The narrative of Deborah and Barak has important lessons that may be applied to modern leadership. When it comes to making the most of a team's capabilities and potential, collaboration and shared leadership are very necessary. Leaders need to be ready to delegate authority to others, acknowledge the special skills of their followers, and create conditions that encourage their personal and professional development. Leaders can unlock the full potential of their teams when they show appreciation for other points of view and work to create an inclusive workplace.

In addition to this, one of the most important attributes for successful collaboration is an open mind and a sense of modesty. It is important for leaders to be open to a variety of points of view, to recognise the significance of the contributions made by others, and to foster fruitful debate. Leaders have the potential to generate creative ideas and reach greater levels of success via true cooperation.

Key Take Aways:

Collaboration and giving people the power to make their own decisions are two crucial leadership methods that enhance engagement among team members and the joint accomplishment of goals. The following is the synergistic effect of various strategies:

Developing an Atmosphere That Encourages Collaboration:

Encourage Open Communication: Do your best to keep the lines of communication open and honest within the group. The conditions for productive cooperation are established when individuals in a team do not feel inhibited in voicing their thoughts and concerns.

Establishing trust is essential to productive teamwork because it serves as the glue that holds everyone together. Display confidence in your team's capabilities and goals and encourage individual members to have confidence in one another as well.

Clearly identify the aims and objectives that are shared by all parties involved. When members of a team are committed to the same objective, they are more likely to cooperate with one another to reach that objective.

To facilitate interactions, you should organise chances for members of the team to collaborate and communicate with one another. This may take the form of group get-togethers, sessions of creative problem-solving, or joint initiatives.

Giving Agency to Third Parties:

Empowering team members through the practise of delegating duties and decision-making authority to other members of the team. People have a better sense of autonomy and motivation when they believe that they have control over the things that they are working on.

Make Sure Your Team Has the required Resources, Information, and Training to Do Their Jobs successfully

Make sure that your team has all of the required resources, information, and training to do their jobs successfully. When members of a team have access to the resources they require, it is much simpler to empower them.

Foster Innovation: Foster an environment that supports and acknowledges creative thinking. Encourage your staff to think of innovative ideas and find inventive ways to solve problems and give them the autonomy to put those ideas into action as they see fit.

To empower people does not mean to abdicate responsibility; rather, it is to offer guidance rather than micromanagement. Provide direction and assistance when it's required but stay away from micromanaging. Have faith in the ability of your team.

The Synergy of Collaborative Efforts and Individual Agency:

The sharing of ideas and different points of view that result from collaborative efforts can lead to increased creative output. It leads to more innovative problem-solving when team members are given the opportunity to submit their thoughts.

Increased Productivity When members of a team are given greater control over their work, they are more likely to take the initiative necessary to increase productivity. Collaboration makes it more likely that their efforts will be in line with the objectives of the team.

Collaboration helps to cultivate a culture of mutual support, in which members of a team lend a helping hand to one another and work to enhance one another's capabilities. This contributes to the formation of a stronger and more cohesive team.

Personal Development When members of a team are given the opportunity to tackle new problems and take on more responsibilities, it can result in personal and professional development, which is to the advantage of both the individuals and the team.

Leadership Development: One strategy for identifying potential leaders within a team is to encourage members of the team to take the initiative in leading certain projects or initiatives.

Accomplishments should be acknowledged and celebrated.

Recognise and honour the accomplishments of each individual team member as well as the accomplishments of the team. Empowerment and collaboration are both strengthened when individuals' contributions and efforts are acknowledged.

Improvement That Is Constant:

Encourage an attitude that views failure as a learning experience. Encourage members of the team to share their comments, pinpoint areas in which they may improve, and act in order to create improvements together.

Leaders could cultivate a dynamic, motivated, and high-achieving team by integrating the concepts of cooperation and empowerment. This synergy fosters innovation, productivity, and a good work environment in which team members feel appreciated and can make a significant effect on the project as a whole.

Chapter 7:

Daniel's Exemplary Character: Leading with Integrity in a Hostile Environment

The Old Testament narrative of Daniel serves as a potent illustration of the significance of maintaining one's moral compass while serving in a position of leadership within a challenging setting. For leaders who are looking for an inspiring example of how to manage hard circumstances while still preserving their ideals, Daniel's unshakable devotion to his principles, even in the face of adversity, offers as an excellent model to look to.

The events that comprise the beginning of Daniel's tale begin when he and his fellow Israelites are kidnapped by the Babylonians and forced to serve in the royal court of King Nebuchadnezzar. Daniel's dedication to God and trust in God's existence are unshaken even though he is currently living in a foreign country with a different culture and set of beliefs. He will not budge from his ideals, and as a result, he is an unshakeable model of integrity that others may model themselves after.

One of the key points in Daniel's journey is when he is presented with an edict issued by monarch Darius that forbids anybody to pray to any god or anyone other than the monarch himself. Daniel's reaction to this decree is one of the defining moments in Daniel's story. Daniel is aware of the tension that exists between this command and his dedication to God, yet he makes the decision to carry on praying to God three times every day regardless of the repercussions. The strength of leadership with integrity in the face of adversity is demonstrated by his steadfast unwillingness to compromise his religious values and his unyielding dedication to upholding those principles.

The impeccable moral fibre and unwavering honesty that Daniel possesses are not ignored. Because to his unwavering dedication to his ideals as well as his talent for dream interpretation, he earns the favour and respect of his captors, including the kings of Babylonia. Daniel's integrity is unshaken even when his contemporaries conspire against him and convince the king to enact an edict prohibiting prayer to any deity other than the monarch. He defies the order and keeps praying to God, even though he knows it puts his life in danger for the sake of his faith.

Daniel is someone who, in addition to possessing high levels of personal integrity, has great leadership abilities in his dealings with other people. When he was functioning as an advisor to the kings of Babylon, he shown both knowledge and judgement by delivering the monarchs intelligent readings of their dreams and providing direction when the kingdom was facing a crisis. Because he is focused on bringing honour and glory to God rather than to himself, his dealings with individuals in positions of power are marked by a profound sense of humility and respect for others.

The honesty and strength of character demonstrated by Daniel in the face of opposition is instructive to us. To begin, those who aspire to positions of authority must possess a robust moral compass and an unyielding dedication to their core ideals, even when confronted with challenges. When faced with adversity, one's genuine character is revealed, and those in positions of authority who can preserve their integrity earn the respect and trust of their followers.

Second, to lead with integrity, one must have the guts to stand up for what is right and the desire to do so regardless of the potential consequences to oneself. It is an encouragement for leaders to keep their convictions and remain steadfast in their principles no matter the difficulties that they may encounter, and Daniel's unwillingness to compromise his faith in the face of hardship serves as an example of how to do so.

In conclusion, the narrative of Daniel demonstrates the significance of humility, wisdom, and insight in effective leadership. Leaders can make wise choices and provide insightful contributions that have a beneficial effect on others around them when they actively seek the advice and guidance of God and rely on his direction.

Key Take Aways:

It can be particularly difficult to lead with integrity in a hostile environment, yet doing so is an essential test of a leader's character and the ideals that guide their actions. When faced with such challenges, upholding your integrity not only demonstrates your commitment to upholding ethical norms, but it also has the potential to motivate others to do the same. The following are some tactics that may be used to lead with integrity in challenging environments:

Always Remain Faithful to Your Principles:

Define your fundamental ethical ideals and values and stick to them. Even when you are confronted with animosity, you should let these guide your decisions and actions.

Communication That Is Both Open and Transparent:

Encourage communication that is both open and candid among your team. Discuss the difficulties and the antagonistic factors openly and urge the others of your team to do the same.

Setting a Good Example:

Show your staff the kind of integrity and ethical behaviour you demand from them, and model it yourself. Everyone will model their behaviour after how you conduct yourself.

Maintain Your Composure and Your Calm:

Environments that are hostile can sometimes elicit strong feelings. Even under challenging circumstances, you should always strive to keep your calm and emotional intelligence. Try to control your impulse to respond.

Establishing trust:

Make it a priority to develop trust among the members of your team. When navigating through a dangerous setting, trust is very necessary. When members of a team trust one another and their leader, it is much simpler for the team to tackle difficult tasks collectively.

Making Decisions Based on Ethics:

Always choose actions that are moral, even in situations where it would be easier to break the rules. Maintaining your integrity will be easier thanks to your dedication to upholding ethical standards, especially under challenging circumstances.

Look for areas of agreement:

In the hostile atmosphere, look for places where you and other people share something in common. Finding common ground in terms of aims or interests can be an effective way to defuse tense situations and open doors to collaboration.

Privacy and discretion:

Maintain the privacy of sensitive information and protect it at all costs. This implies that you can be trusted and can assist you in navigating potentially difficult environments while maintaining discretion.

Put Your Attention on Long-Term Objectives:

Always make sure that you are keeping your focus on the long-term objectives and the vision that you have for your team or organisation. When confronted with antagonism, adopting this point of view can assist you in putting things into perspective and determining what matters most.

Create a Record and Document:

It may be required to keep a record of any interactions or hostile activities that take place in certain situations for legal or accountability reasons. Make sure that you act ethically and in accordance with the law when doing so.

Try to Find Help:

Don't be afraid to ask your mentors, peers, or trusted advisers for advice or direction; they are there to help you. They can offer helpful insights as well as a different point of view on how to handle the scenario.

Always Practise Good Self-Care:

It is necessary to pay attention to both your bodily and mental well-being. When you're in a hostile situation, stress may take its toll, so it's important to make taking care of yourself a top priority.

Resistance to harm:

Gain the ability to overcome obstacles and failures by developing your resilience. In the face of challenging circumstances, resilience will enable you to maintain your dedication to your values and goals.

Concerns for Both Your Safety and the Law:

Safety should always come first, and all legal criteria should be met. When required, communicate with legal professionals and law enforcement personnel if the antagonism offers any threats, whether they be physical or legal.

Determine When You Need to Take a Stand:

Even while it's necessary to try to find common ground and negotiate a hostile environment diplomatically, there may be moments when you must take a position for your beliefs and integrity that is principled.

It is a test of both character and leadership to be able to lead with integrity in a challenging setting. Even while it may not be simple, doing so may inspire others, lead to a workplace that is more ethical, and eventually result in an environment that is more pleasant and productive.

Chapter 8:

Ruth's Loyalty and Servant Leadership

The book of Ruth in the Old Testament provides us with an outstanding illustration of steadfastness and leadership via service. The unyielding allegiance that Ruth shown towards Naomi, her mother-in-law, and the selfless acts of service that she performed for Naomi offer invaluable insights into the nature of great leadership, which is founded on devotion and compassion.

Naomi and her family are forced to leave their hometown of Bethlehem because of the severe famine, and this is the setting for the events that make up the tale of Ruth. Ruth, a Moabite widow, makes the selfless decision to stay at Naomi's side, displaying an incredible level of devotion and commitment. Her well-known saying, "Where you go, I will go; where you stay, I will stay," encapsulates the intensity of her commitment and the selflessness with which she treats her connection with Naomi. "Where you go, I will go; where you stay, I will stay."

The commitment shown by Ruth extends beyond simple words. As a leader who prioritises others' needs over her own, she makes it her mission to find Naomi suitable means of assistance and care. She demonstrates a sense of humility and a strong work ethic by offering to glean in the fields in order to produce food for both of them. The fact that she is ready to serve shows the concept of servant leadership at its core, and it indicates the depth of her dedication to Naomi's health and happiness.

Ruth draws the notice of Boaz, a prominent character who also happens to be a relative of Naomi's late husband, while they are both working in the fields. Ruth's remarkable character, as well as her actions of devotion and generosity, are acknowledged by Boaz. He compliments her on the generous acts that she has performed and offers her his protection and assistance. The fact that Boaz saw Ruth's talents as a servant leader and commended her for them further emphasises the need of humility, loyalty, and compassion in effective leadership.

The narrative of Ruth provides us with several important insights on faithfulness and leadership based on service. To begin, one of the most essential qualities of a leader is their loyalty. They can get through challenging moments together thanks to Ruth's unfailing dedication to Naomi, which establishes a deep link of trust and support between the two of them. Leaders who develop an environment of trust and cooperation by honouring their commitments and sincerely caring for the well-being of their followers can create an atmosphere that is conducive to both trust and collaboration.

Second, servant leadership is characterised by an absence of self-interest and an openness to serving the needs of others. Gleaning the fields is one of the ways that Ruth demonstrates both her humility and her commitment to providing for the requirements of the people that she cares for. The health and development of their followers is of the utmost importance to servant leaders, who look for ways to inspire and encourage their followers.

In addition to this, Ruth's narrative emphasises the value of acknowledging and being grateful for the contributions made by others. The fact that Boaz recognises Ruth's faithfulness and traits of servant leadership improves her status and helps to cultivate an atmosphere in which she may fully realise her potential. Leaders that take the time to notice and appreciate the contributions made by their followers contribute to the growth of an appreciative culture and provide their followers the ability to realise their full potential.

The narrative of Ruth is still used to motivate and encourage leaders in modern times, and it serves as a useful reminder of the power of loyalty and servant leadership. Ruth exhibits the attributes that are necessary for effective leadership via her unyielding dedication to Naomi and her unselfish acts of devotion to others. Leaders that place a high priority on loyalty, humility, and compassion are able to cultivate an atmosphere in which their followers may flourish individually, and the group as a whole can achieve success.

Key Take Aways:

When skilfully integrated, the leadership ideas of loyalty and servant leadership may provide an environment that is encouraging of teamwork and cohesive among its members. This can be a positive outcome for any organisation. The following exemplifies the relationship between loyalty and servant leadership:

Faithfulness:

Loyalty to One's Team: Leaders that place a high importance on loyalty work to instil a sense of dedication and companionship among the members of their teams. The members of the team have a powerful sense of belonging, and they are dedicated to the leader as well as the aims of the group.

Building Trust: Loyalty helps build trust between the team leader and the members of the team. When members of a team have faith that their leader is committed to looking out for their welfare and ensuring their success, a foundation of trust is established, which is essential for efficient teamwork.

Support and loyalty are given and received in equal measure. A leader who demonstrates loyalty to the members in their team will motivate that devotion to be returned. It is more probable that members of a team will support their boss as well as each other, so establishing an environment at work that is cohesive and supportive.

Stability and Consistency: Loyalty frequently translates into both qualities. Even in difficult times, the members of the team are certain that their leader will continue to help them in any way possible.

Leadership via Service:

Putting Others Before Yourself: One trait of servant leaders is putting the requirements and welfare of their team members ahead of their own. They want to encourage and facilitate the growth of others so that they can realise their greatest potential.

Empowerment refers to the process by which servant leaders give team members the authority to make decisions, accept responsibility for their job, and contribute to the overall success of the team. The members of the team will develop a sense of ownership in the project because of this empowerment.

Listening Actively: A trait of servant leaders is the ability to actively listen to the concerns, thoughts, and criticisms of their team members. They develop a sense of trust and worth among the members of the team by being attentive and responsive to one another.

Personal Development: Servant leaders are those that are dedicated to the development of their team members both personally and professionally. They provide possibilities for learning and growth, as well as assistance and mentorship to those who are interested.

The Mutually Reinforcing Relationship Between Loyalty and Servant Leadership:

Trust Is Increased When Loyalty and Servant Leadership Work Together Loyalty and servant leadership work together to produce a high degree of trust within the team. The members of the team have faith in their leader's dedication to looking out for their interests and fostering their growth, which in turn reinforces the sense of loyalty those members have towards their leader.

The leader and the members of the team can provide mutual support for one another when the leader demonstrates both loyalty and servant leadership. The leader encourages the development and accomplishments of team members, and the members of the team, in turn, demonstrate loyalty and support for the leader.

Open and Honest Communication is Encouraged by Using Both of These tactics Together The combination of these two tactics supports open and honest communication. Because the members of the team are confident that their leader has their best interests in mind, they do not feel uncomfortable voicing their opinions and concerns.

Positive Team Dynamics are fostered by the synergy that exists between loyalty and servant leadership. It is more probable that members of a team will successfully interact with one another, work towards common goals, and establish an environment at work that is supportive and cooperative.

Commitment Over Time: The combination of these two strategies encourages commitment over time. It is more probable that members of a team will continue to be loyal to the organisation and its leader, which contributes to the continued success and stability of the organisation.

In a nutshell, the combination of faithfulness and servant leadership generates a potent force that increases trust, mutual support, and collaborative efforts among members of a group. It results in a working atmosphere in which members of the team have the sense that they are respected, empowered, and devoted to the leader's vision as well as the organization's goals.

Chapter 9:

Joshua and the Battle of Jericho: Leading with Boldness and Faith

The book of Joshua has a narrative titled "Joshua and the Battle of Jericho," which teaches readers crucial lessons about becoming a courageous and faithful leader. Joshua's persistent belief in God's promises, his courage in the face of seemingly insurmountable circumstances, and his strategic leadership give motivation for leaders who wish to overcome problems and accomplish amazing wins. Joshua was the leader of the Israelites during the conquest of the Promised Land.

Joshua, who was Moses's chosen successor, was given the responsibility of guiding the Israelites into the land that had been promised to them. Their first significant challenge is the walled city of Jericho, which is an adversary of high calibre. On the other side, God gives Joshua a divine guarantee that He will give them control of the city that they have been attacking. Joshua sets off on a trip with this pledge, which will put his leadership to the test and demand that he maintains steadfast trust.

Joshua's leadership is distinguished by courage and a profound dependence on God. Joshua led the Israelites for forty years. He is wise enough to know that human might, and cunning are not the only factors that determine success; heavenly providence also plays a role. Joshua exemplifies his faith by obeying God's commands, even though some of them are counterintuitive and go against the accepted practises of the military. He then marches the Israelites around the city of Jericho for six days straight, and on the seventh day, when they have marched around the city seven times, they begin yelling and blowing their trumpets. The Israelites can declare victory after the miraculous collapse of the city walls of Jericho.

Important life lessons concerning the need of leading with faith and confidence may be learned from Joshua's leadership. To begin, those in leadership roles need to have the intestinal fortitude to force themselves out of their comfort zones and take risks. Joshua's unique approach of circling the city may have looked unreasonable, but his steadfast conviction in God's leadership inspired him to lead with confidence even when it was counterintuitive. It is possible for leaders to inspire their people to achieve amazing achievements if they have the courage to disrupt the status quo and take calculated risks.

Second, the narrative of Joshua highlights the significance of maintaining steadfast faith during challenging circumstances. Joshua's faith in God's promises enabled him to confidently lead the Israelites through the battle of Jericho, despite the considerable difficulties that were posed. It is possible for leaders to unlock incredible potential and resiliency in their organisations if they cultivate a culture of faith and encourage their staff to trust in something greater than themselves.

In addition, Joshua's leadership highlights the need of strategic thought and planning, which is an important point. Although religion played a significant part, strategic military manoeuvres were also an important component. The capacity of Joshua to analyse the situation, formulate a strategy, and carry out the plan with pinpoint accuracy underscores the significance of integrating spiritual conviction with worldly experience. Leaders who can successfully manage difficult difficulties and lead their teams to victory are those who combine faith-based beliefs with strategic thinking.

The narrative of Joshua and the Battle of Jericho is a potent reminder that courage, faith, and smart leadership can all lead to great results, and it serves as a striking example of all three. It is possible for leaders to inspire their teams to triumph over challenges that at first glance appear to be insurmountable if they have the guts to take the initiative, steadfast trust in their mission, and the capacity to design and carry out strategic plans.

Key Take Aways:

An approach to leadership known as bold and faith-based leadership is taking decisive and brave acts while simultaneously retaining a deep conviction in the capabilities of one's team and the positive results that will result from those efforts. This is how these two characteristics complement one another:

The courage to:

Making Brave Decisions Brave leaders are ready to make difficult decisions, especially when such decisions contain risks and uncertainty. They are not afraid to venture outside of their comfort zones and accept risks that have been carefully weighed in order to realise their goals.

Innovating new solutions to problems is something that daring leaders actively push their teams to do. They motivate their staff to think creatively and critically, and to question the established order.

Leadership via Vision: Courageous leaders frequently possess a distinct and aspirational vision for the future. They are not afraid to go for lofty objectives and motivate their team to strive towards achieving such objectives.

Confidence is a trait that is contagious among courageous leaders, who in turn instil confidence in their followers. The unflinching faith that they have in their own capabilities and the opportunities before them may be a morale booster for the team.

Resilience: Bold leaders could bounce back quickly from defeat and difficult circumstances. They do not allow challenges to deter them but rather view them as chances for personal development and growth.

Have faith in:

Belief in Other People: Leaders who have faith trust and have confidence in the capabilities of the people on their teams. They are certain that their team have the necessary abilities and willpower to fulfil the goals that have been established.

Optimism: Even when confronted with difficult circumstances, faithful leaders have a constructive and hopeful attitude on the issue. They inspire those on their team to view challenges as only transitory obstacles on the way to achieving their goals.

Faith-filled leaders invest their followers with the authority to act independently and make choices on behalf of the team. They foster the growth of their team while providing the necessary support and resources for success in the endeavours they undertake.

Vision and Purpose: Devout leaders have a strong and abiding connection to their own visions and purposes. They establish a sense of common purpose and a sense of shared vision in their team by communicating the vision they have.

Encouragement and Support Faith-filled leaders make it a priority to provide their teams with regular support and encouragement. They provide encouragement, inspiration, and assurance to the members of the team.

The Complementarity of Fearlessness and Belief:

Leadership that is Characterised by Boldness and Faith Boldness and faith working together produce leadership that is daring. Faith in the skills of the team and the accomplishment of the objective ultimately motivates people to take courageous acts.

Inspiration: The team is inspired to accept challenges and strive towards ambitious goals with dedication and enthusiasm thanks to the boldness and faith demonstrated by each individual member.

Positive Aspects of Taking Risks Bravery and faith inspire individuals to take calculated risks. Because they have trust in the potential of the team to prevail despite the challenges they face, leaders are ready to take risks.

Both Resilience and Perseverance are Strengthened When These Traits Are Combined: The combination of these traits increases the leader's ability to be resilient and persevere. Even in the face of challenges, they have not wavered in their conviction that the squad can achieve its goals.

Leadership that Empowers Followers Brave leaders who have trust in their vision encourage their teams to take ownership of their work, make decisions, and steer the organisation in the direction of its goals.

In conclusion, leading with boldness and faith is a dynamic style to leadership that entails taking bold and measured choices while keeping unshakable trust in the capabilities of the team and the great outcomes that may be achieved through their combined efforts. This combination has the potential to excite and drive the team, leading to outstanding achievement.

Chapter 10:

Esther's Influence: Leadership through Diplomacy and Risk-taking

The book of Esther in the Old Testament is a great example of amazing leadership abilities such as diplomacy and taking calculated risks. The bold deeds that Esther committed and the smart diplomacy that she exercised in the face of grave peril provide an illuminating model for leaders who are tasked with navigating difficult circumstances and pushing for positive change.

After capturing the attention of King Xerxes, Esther, a Jewish orphan, is elevated to the position of queen of Persia. Esther is a member of a religious group that is discriminated against and persecuted in society, but the king has no idea about this. Esther is put in a position where she must choose between life and death when the evil Haman hatches a scheme to wipe out all of the Jews living in the realm. She muster's up the bravery to use her position and influence for the greater good, despite the inherent dangers involved.

When Esther meticulously develops her strategy, her ability to exercise leadership through diplomatic means becomes readily apparent. She invites the monarch and Haman to a series of feasts, deftly utilising these meetings as occasions to disclose Haman's nefarious intentions and beg for her people's survival. Recognising the significance of timing and obtaining the favour of the king, she does so by inviting the king and Haman to a series of banquets. The fact that Esther was able to traverse the complexities of court politics and win the compassion of the king by communicating in a way that was both convincing and diplomatic demonstrates that she had excellent leadership acumen.

In addition to this, Esther's leadership is exemplified by taking risks while keeping the big picture in mind. She is aware that her people would perish if she does nothing, so she makes the courageous decision to disclose her Jewish heritage to the monarch. She does this because she knows that inactivity will result in the death of her people. This bold gesture exemplifies her willingness to put herself in harm's way for the greater good, and it illustrates her dedication to fighting for justice and rescuing her people.

The narrative of Esther teaches important lessons about leadership. To begin, the art of diplomacy is a potent instrument for political leaders. Esther's ability to influence important decision-makers and alter the trajectory of events is made possible by her strategic approach, her capacity for building relationships, and her compelling communication abilities. Diplomacy is an essential talent for leaders, and those who make it a part of their development are better able to negotiate complicated relationships, form alliances, and advocate for their objectives.

Second, the narrative of Esther demonstrates the significance of taking measured risks when one is in a leadership position. Going outside one's comfort zone and meeting challenges head-on are sometimes necessary steps for making substantial changes and advancing one's goals. Leaders are inspired to take calculated risks for the service of a bigger cause by Esther's courage to speak up, despite the fact that she may have put her own safety in jeopardy by doing so.

The story of Esther also highlights the importance of having empathy for others and speaking up for what you believe in. The profound care and concern that Esther has for the welfare of her people is the driving force behind her mission to save them. Leaders that exhibit empathy and advocate for the requirements of underrepresented groups or causes can instil in their followers a sense of belonging and motivate them to band together in support of a common goal.

The narrative of Esther and her ability to lead via diplomacy and taking risks provides an enduring model for leaders who want to bring about positive change in hard situations. Leaders can manage complicated scenarios, inspire others, and make an influence that will last by embracing diplomacy, taking risks in a controlled manner, and pushing for justice.

Key Take Aways:

Leadership via diplomacy and risk-taking is a dynamic leadership technique that entails skilfully negotiating complicated situations and making courageous judgements. This type of leadership requires bold decision-making as well as the ability to navigate complex situations. This is how these two characteristics complement one another:

A word about diplomacy:

Diplomatic leaders are great communicators, and effective communication is one of the keys to their success. They can communicate their message in a way that is both clear and convincing, whether they are speaking to other members of the team, stakeholders, or external parties.

Resolution of Conflict: Diplomatic leaders are experts in finding peaceful solutions to contentious issues. They could resolve disagreements, locate areas of agreement, and keep the peace within the group or organisation.

Negotiation is a frequent part of the diplomatic process, and diplomatic leaders could reach agreements that are to the mutual benefit of all parties involved. They look for solutions that benefit both parties.

Empathy is a trait that is essential for successful diplomats, since it allows them to comprehend the experiences and feelings of others. They are able to connect with other members of the team as well as stakeholders, which helps to cultivate trust and positive connections.

Sensitivity to Culture: Diplomatic leaders in varied contexts are sensitive to cultural variations and modify their approach to work effectively with persons from a variety of backgrounds.

Taking the Risk:

Having the Courage to Make big judgements Leaders that are willing to take risks have the courage to make big judgements, especially when faced with uncertainty. They are not scared to question the way things are currently done and are open to new ideas.

Creativity and new ideas are fostered by those who are willing to take risks. They motivate their team to consider novel ideas and techniques, which ultimately results in the development of ground-breaking solutions.

Visionary leadership is exemplified by those who are willing to take calculated risks. They inspire their team to attain ambitious objectives by setting lofty targets for the group.

Ability to Adapt: Those who take risks can adjust and remain flexible in the face of ever-changing conditions. They perceive obstacles as chances for personal development and advancement.

Resilience is a trait shared by courageous leaders, who are also persistent. They continue to be dedicated to their mission despite the obstacles that have been placed in their path.

The Complementarity of Diplomacy and Cautious Action:

Effective Decision-Making Effective decision-making may be achieved by a combination of diplomatic manoeuvring and calculated risk-taking. Leaders that are skilled in diplomacy make use of their communication abilities to explain the reasoning behind risky actions, so getting buy-in and understanding.

Reducing the Risk of Conflict Diplomatic leaders have the ability to reduce the likelihood of disputes occuring as a result of risk-taking actions by clearly conveying the advantages of those decisions and addressing concerns.

Diplomatic abilities are in helpful when lobbying for support and resources that are important for endeavours that involve taking risks. Leaders could forge alliances and obtain the necessary support by doing so.

The team is inspired to accept change, to take chances that are appropriate to the situation, and to achieve ambitious goals because of the mix of diplomacy and risk-taking. The members of the team have faith in their leader's capacity to successfully handle change.

Problem Solving Leaders that use diplomacy with their teams are better able to collaborate with other members of the team to find solutions to challenges that may be brought about by decisions including risk. It inspires collaboration among group members and the sharing of ideas.

Management of Crises: Diplomatic abilities help leaders handle crises with tact, preserve confidence, and find solutions when taking risks doesn't go as planned.

In a nutshell, competent management of both the people and the choices that drive an organisation is required for exercising leadership through the use of diplomacy and taking calculated risks. In order to inspire and motivate a team to produce extraordinary outcomes, it combines excellent communication, conflict resolution, and negotiation with bold, visionary decision-making, flexibility, and resilience.

Chapter 11:

Paul's Transformation: From Persecutor to Apostle of the Early Church

The narrative of Paul's journey from a persecutor of the early Christian church to one of its most powerful apostles is a tribute to the power of human development, resilience, and redemption. Paul went from being a persecutor of the early Christian church to becoming one of its most important apostles. The trip that Paul took could serve as a motivating example for leaders who want to get over their own struggles, be open to new experiences, and have a beneficial effect on the world.

Before he was converted, Paul, who was also known as Saul, was a fervent opponent of Christians and a persecutor of the church. Because he saw the early Christian movement as a danger to the Jewish practises and ideas he had been up with, he worked aggressively for its eradication. On the way to Damascus, he had an encounter with a supernatural insight, which caused his life to take a drastic turn for the better. This experience with the resurrected Jesus Christ brought about a dramatic shift in his worldview and launched him on the path towards personal transformation.

The transition that takes place in Paul is characterised by several important shifts in his life. The first thing that happens is that he has a total change of heart and begins to follow the example set by Jesus Christ. Because of this life-altering encounter, he decides to forsake his prior deeds and beliefs and instead devotes his life to following Christ's teachings. The ability of Paul to reject his own deeply set ideas and embrace a new path exemplifies the power of personal growth and the possibility for significant transformation.

Second, the change of Paul is exemplified by characteristics such as resiliency and endurance. Paul's faith and dedication to preaching the gospel of Christ remain unshaken in spite of the countless obstacles and difficulties he has had to overcome throughout his life, such as being imprisoned, subjected to persecution, and encountering resistance from both religious and secular authorities. His tenacity in the face of hardship may serve as a model for leaders who, on their own paths to change, meet challenges along the way.

Additionally, Paul's metamorphosis enables him to become a prominent apostle and a major role in the early Christian church. This is a direct result of Paul's conversion. He embarks on a lengthy missionary journey around the Mediterranean area with the purpose of disseminating the teachings of Christ and building Christian communities. The leadership qualities that set Paul apart are his fervour, his eloquence, and his unflinching commitment to the task at hand. The fact that he was able to go from being a persecutor to an apostle is an example of the ability of individuals to not only triumph over their own history but also become agents of good change and transformation in the lives of others.

Lessons in effective leadership may be gleaned from Paul's experience. In the first place, it highlights the significance of one's own capacity for change and development. Leaders who are ready to confront their own prejudices, challenge their preconceived views, and embrace change have the ability to inspire people around them and establish a culture that is committed to continual growth.

Second, the transition that Paul underwent exemplifies the significance of resiliency and tenacity in the role of a leader. The path leading to increased personal and professional development is almost never devoid of obstacles and roadblocks. Leaders who have the fortitude to triumph over adversity and the persistence to remain steadfast in their commitment to their goal could inspire others and make a major influence.

In addition, the tale of Paul highlights the possibility of atonement and the capacity to make a good effect, even though one may have made mistakes or fallen short in the past. Not only can leaders improve their own lives, but also the lives of the people they are responsible for if they are ready to reflect, learn from their experiences, and actively pursue chances for growth.

The life of Paul, who went from being a persecutor of the early church to becoming one of its apostles, is a compelling example of one's ability to undergo transformation, find atonement, and experience personal development. Leaders may discover the motivation they need to embrace transformation, demonstrate resilience, and make an effect that will last in their own circles of influence by looking to his example.

Key Take Aways:

The process of evolving and adapting one's leadership style and approach to suit the changing demands and difficulties of an organisation, team, or environment is referred to as transformation in leadership. This process can take place over the course of one's career as a leader. It frequently requires a transition away from classic or conventional techniques of leadership towards methods that are more contemporary, flexible, and adaptable. The following are important components of the transformative leadership:

The ability to adapt to new situations and circumstances is a trait shared by transformational leaders. They make it a habit to regularly evaluate the requirements of their company or team and to adapt their management style accordingly.

Conceptualisation of a Clear and Convincing Vision for the Future Visionary thinking is a common trait among transformational leaders. They motivate people to work together towards a similar goal by communicating this vision to them and inspiring them to do so.

Transformational leadership fosters an environment that is conducive to creativity as well as innovative approaches to resolving issues. Leaders foster an environment in which members of the team have the perception that they have the authority to produce fresh ideas and solutions.

Empowerment is a key characteristic of transformational leaders, who encourage their teams to assume personal responsibility for the job being done. They give the independence as well as the resources that are required for success.

These leaders inspire and drive their teams to accomplish amazing outcomes, and they are an inspiration to others. They inspire others to follow their lead and cultivate a feeling of common purpose and ideals.

Emotional Intelligence Transformational leaders have a high level of emotional intelligence, which allows them to understand and control their own emotions as well as the emotions of others around them. They make the working environment upbeat and encouraging for everyone.

Transformational leaders are dedicated to their own personal and professional development, which requires continuous learning. They foster an environment where learning and development are encouraged for all members of the team.

Resilience: These leaders can bounce back quickly from defeat and difficult circumstances. Even when faced with difficult circumstances, they have a good attitude and remain steadfast in their commitment to their mission.

Collaboration is a key component of transformational leadership, which places an emphasis on cooperation. Leaders are responsible for constructing teams that are robust and cohesive and encouraging support between members.

Ethical Considerations Transformational leaders make judgements that are ethical and consider the moral repercussions of their actions. They place a premium on morality and honesty in their actions.

Transformational leaders are adept at managing change inside their organisations, which is one of their primary responsibilities. They are aware of the significance of change and aid their teams so that they may effectively manage it.

Resolution of disputes Skilled leaders in change have the ability to handle disputes and address difficulties within their teams or organisations in a way that is diplomatic and productive.

Measuring Success: These leaders frequently evaluate success not just in terms of traditional metrics, but also by the influence on the culture of the organisation, innovation, and flexibility as well.

The ability to communicate in a clear and concise manner is a fundamental component of transformative leadership. Leaders are those that engage in open and honest discussion with their teams, and they make sure their people are aware of their vision, goals, and expectations.

Perspective on the Long-Term Transformational leaders always have an eye on the big picture. They are dedicated to the long-term development and accomplishments of their organisation or group.

The process of transformation in leadership is an ongoing one that is a response to the continuously shifting terrain of the corporate world. It requires a dedication to one's own personal development and adaptation, as well as a concentration on motivating and enabling others to realise their greatest potential in life. In the long run, it results in an organisation or team that is more inventive, resilient, and dynamic.

Chapter 12:

Peter's Leadership in the Early Christian Community: Learning from Mistakes

Peter, who was also known by his Greek name Simon Peter, is often regarded as one of the most influential people in the early Christian community. His road to leadership has been marked by exceptional strengths as well as humbling blunders, which makes his tale an invaluable source of lessons for leaders who are on the path towards development, learning, and resilience.

When Jesus called him to be one of the twelve disciples, Peter's journey with Jesus officially got under way. Throughout the entirety of Jesus' mission, Peter demonstrated tremendous zeal and faithfulness, frequently assuming a position of leadership among the disciples. However, Peter's leadership was also distinguished by times of impetuous behaviour and personal shortcomings on his part. Those moments are what make his leadership unique.

Peter's denial of Jesus on the night before Jesus was arrested is one of the Peter's errors that is most well-known to the public. Peter, who had before professed his unshakeable commitment to Jesus, eventually gave in to his fears and denied any relationship with Jesus on three separate occasions. This instance of helplessness serves as a potent reminder that even the most dedicated and talented leaders are prone to making errors in judgement from time to time.

Despite this, Peter's narrative does not conclude with him being unsuccessful. Following Jesus' resurrection, Peter goes through a period of deep self-development and transformation. He grows as a person because of his experiences, coming to terms with his weaknesses and eventually becoming a key leader in the early Christian society. When leaders go through difficult times or make mistakes in their own travels, they may acquire invaluable lessons from Peter's humility, perseverance, and readiness to learn from such experiences.

Peter's capacity to reflect on his actions, identify areas for improvement, and mature as a result is an essential component of his leadership. In the aftermath of his denial of Jesus, Peter had a transformative encounter with Jesus on the beaches of the Sea of Galilee. In this moment, they are reconciled. Jesus reconciles Peter to himself and gives him the task of shepherding the flock that he has created. Peter could become a more compassionate, empathic, and successful leader because of his willingness to embrace this second opportunity and his dedication to learning from his errors.

The path that Peter took teaches us another important lesson about leadership: the value of humility. Peter acknowledges his limits and places his trust in the grace and direction that God provides, even though he was formerly in a prominent position among the disciples. Because of his humble nature, he can gain knowledge from other people, seek advice, and establish solid ties within the early Christian community. Leaders who practise humility are better able to foster an environment that values open communication, ongoing education, and teamwork.

In addition to that, the narrative of Peter demonstrates the need of resilience in leadership. In spite of the many mistakes, he had made in the past, Peter developed into a powerful and prominent leader who was instrumental in the expansion and formation of the early Christian church. The transformational potential of resilience in leadership is demonstrated by his capacity to recover quickly from failures, seize chances for personal growth, and lead with a refreshed sense of mission.

The tale of Peter's leadership in the early Christian community offers us a valuable lesson: that mistakes and setbacks are not what constitute a leader. Instead, the capacity to develop from one's experiences, to lead with humility and resiliency, and to learn from one's mistakes is what truly defines a leader's character. Leaders may foster a mentality of continual learning, personal growth, and grace for themselves and others by accepting the lessons that can be learned from Peter's path and applying them.

Key Take Aways:

Recognising and gaining wisdom from one's errors is an essential component of both personal and professional development. The reality is that making mistakes is an inevitable part of living, but if you approach them with the appropriate mentality, you can turn them into important chances for learning and growth. To properly learn from one's errors, the following fundamental concepts should be adhered to:

Acceptance, as well as Responsibility:

Recognise the error without assigning blame or taking a defensive stance. Recognise and accept that making errors is an inevitable aspect of the human experience.

Reflection Upon Oneself:

Spend some time thinking about the error you made. Ask yourself what went wrong, what led to the error, and what might have been done better in order to get to the bottom of the situation.

Determine the Underlying Factors:

Investigate further in order to have a better understanding of the underlying circumstances that contributed to the error. Were there problems with the system, breakdowns in communication, or human faults that led to this?

Look for Responses:

Request comments from your coworkers, mentors, or bosses, since they may offer some insights into the error you made. Perspectives from the outside can be quite helpful in gaining insights.

Establish a Course of Action:

Create a strategy that will correct the error and stop it from happening again in the future. This strategy must include definite measures that may be carried out.

Make the Necessary Adjustments:

Implement your strategy and make it a reality. Put in place the required alterations and modifications to save yourself from making the same error again.

Ensure Your Goals Are SMART:

You may measure your progress towards avoiding making the same mistakes in the future by setting objectives that are SMART, which stands for specific, measurable, attainable, relevant, and time-bound.

Look for Ways to Improve Constantly:

Adopt a "growth mindset," and make a commitment to your own continuous progress. Make the most of your failures by viewing them as learning opportunities for both your personal and professional lives.

Accept the Need for Resilience:

Gain the ability to bounce back quickly from defeat by strengthening your resilience. Mistakes may be emotionally taxing, but having a mentality that is resilient can help you push through these challenges.

Please Have Mercy on Yourself:

Be compassionate towards oneself and always show kindness to yourself. Keep in mind that errors are a part of the human experience and that they present a chance for learning and development.

Discuss the Lessons:

If it's acceptable, talk to your coworkers or members of your team about the things you've learnt from the mistakes you've made. This has the potential to foster a culture of continuous growth and learning inside your organisation.

Stop the Culture of Pointing Fingers:

Foster an environment in which errors are seen more as learning experiences and chances for personal development than as justifications for assigning blame. Develop a culture in which people feel at ease admitting when they are wrong and supporting them in doing so.

Maintain a Record of:

Keep a journal of your failures and the things you've taken away from them. This might be a helpful reference for the future, as well as a reminder of how much you've grown as a person.

Keep a Low Profile:

Keep in mind that there is no one who is perfect. You may keep your mind open to new information and remain attentive to comments by maintaining a modest attitude.

Put Your Knowledge to Use:

Make use of the experience and insight you've obtained as a result of your past failures in future endeavours. Make use of your experiences in a proactive manner so that you may improve your decision-making and avoid making the same mistakes again.

The process of gaining knowledge from one's own errors is an ongoing one that helps to one's professional and personal growth. The adoption of this approach with the appropriate mentality and a dedication to progress can result in improved decision-making, problem-solving, and personal development.

Chapter 13:

Prudence and Wisdom: Lessons from Proverbs for Effective Leadership

In the Bible, the book of Proverbs provides a wealth of information and direction for leaders who are striving to build prudence and wisdom in their path as leaders. The book of Proverbs contains ageless truths as well as ideas that may be applied in everyday life to improve decision-making, cultivate good relationships, and encourage successful leadership.

Prudence is one of the most important qualities that is emphasised throughout the book of Proverbs. Prudence may be described as the capacity to exercise good judgement and make smart decisions. Prudent leaders are thoughtful in their actions, evaluate the ramifications of their judgements, and consider the influence their choices will have on their followers and organisations over the long run.

The use of one's knowledge and experience in the context of decision making is one definition of wisdom, which is closely tied to prudence. When discussing qualities necessary for effective leadership, wisdom refers to having an in-depth knowledge of human nature, the capacity to see beyond the obvious, and a dedication to receiving advice from reliable sources.

The book of Proverbs reminds us that successful leaders are those who incorporate caution and wisdom into their methods for making decisions. They take the prospective consequences into thorough consideration, weigh the dangers against the potential advantages, and seek the advice of others. These types of leaders are less likely to be misled by emotions that only have a short-term impact or to be motivated exclusively by their own personal interests. Instead, they place an emphasis on the well-being of others and make decisions that are congruent with their core beliefs and long-term goals.

In addition, the book of Proverbs places a strong emphasis on the role that humility plays in the development of wisdom and discretion. Leaders who are humble enough to confess their shortcomings, accept responsibility for their errors, and maintain a teachable attitude cultivate an atmosphere that is conducive to personal development and promotes teamwork. When leaders exhibit humility, they are able to tap into the collective knowledge of their teams, so gaining access to a wider variety of viewpoints and ideas.

Additionally, the need of clear and concise communication in authoritative roles is emphasised throughout the Proverbs. The ability of leaders to inspire, motivate, and establish trust in their followers comes from their ability to speak in a cautious and smart manner. They are meticulous with their choice of language, always stating the truth in a nice and kind manner. Leaders may cultivate an environment that is respectful and conducive to open communication by engaging in active listening and taking into account the points of view of those around them.

In addition to this, the book of Proverbs emphasises the significance of honesty and morality in leadership roles. The confidence and allegiance of followers is earned by leaders who conduct themselves in a manner that is honest, transparent, and morally upright. They are aware that their deeds speak more loudly than their words, and they try to lead by setting an example.

The lessons of Proverbs provide leaders who are looking to acquire prudence and wisdom in their approach to leadership with counsel that may be used in real-world situations. Leaders are able to make more educated decisions, develop healthier relationships, and motivate people to grow and thrive when they adopt these ideas and put them into practise.

Key Take Aways:

When it comes to leadership, making decisions, and one's own personal development, prudence and wisdom are two separate attributes that are yet connected and play crucial roles. Let's look at the contrasts between them, as well as how they compliment one another:

Reasonable care:

Making Decisions with Caution Being prudent requires making decisions in a deliberate and cautious manner. Before acting on something, prudent people carefully weigh the advantages and disadvantages of the situation.

Evaluation of Risk: Being prudent necessitates doing an analysis of the prospective advantages and disadvantages of various courses of action. It entails making an analysis of the circumstance that is both realistic and logical.

Long-Term Perspective Wise people typically adopt a long-term viewpoint, which requires them to consider not just the immediate repercussions of their choices but also the effects those choices will have in the longer term.

Prudence is a quality that frequently goes hand in hand with practising responsible stewardship. Leaders who use sound judgement carefully manage their organisations' resources, money, and assets to preserve and increase their worth over the long term.

A Strict Adherence to the Rules and Norms: Caution is often associated with a strict adherence to the rules, norms, and best practises that have been developed to reduce potential dangers and preserve order.

Knowledge:

Comprehending Everything It is necessary to have a profound and all-encompassing comprehension of human nature, life, and the universe in order to be wise. It is frequently connected with years of experience as well as an expansive worldview.

Wise people can make ethical and sensible decisions because they have developed excellent judgement. They can look at the situation in its whole and consider the ethical and moral implications of the choices they make.

Empathy and the ability to control one's emotions are two components that are frequently involved in the development of wisdom. Intelligent people can control their sentiments and comprehend the emotions and requirements of others.

Effective Problem-Solving: Effective problem-solving and the capacity to develop novel solutions to difficult problems are both connected to wisdom.

Making Decisions with a Clear Head and a Full Heart Wise choices are frequently arrived at by striking a balance between the logical and the emotional, considering both the mind and the heart.

The Complementarity of Caution and Understanding:

Making judgements That Are Balanced Good leaders combine prudence and wisdom to make judgements that are balanced. These decisions take into account both the practical ramifications of a situation as well as the ethical and moral components of that scenario.

Long-Term Ethical Leadership is the consequence of making prudent judgements with a focus on the long term while being led by wisdom. This type of decision-making produces long-term ethical leadership. When making decisions, astute leaders consider the impact those decisions will have not just on their organisation but also on the people who have a stake in the organisation and on society as a whole.

Resilience: When leaders are confronted with difficulties and defeats, wisdom can assist them in maintaining their resilience. When faced with difficulty, prudent individuals ensure that their answer is well deliberated upon.

Management of Risk That Works Prudent leaders are able to manage risks successfully, but smart leaders grasp the larger implications of those risks, such as the influence they have on relationships and reputation.

Allocating Resources Being prudent in the management of resources and being led by wisdom both guarantee that resources are allotted in a way that is beneficial to the organisation and its mission in the most ethical and meaningful way possible.

Resolution of Conflict Skilled leaders are competent at resolving disagreements and developing solutions that are advantageous to both parties involved. The use of sound judgement guarantees that the proposed solutions are both workable and long-term.

Prudence and wisdom are two distinct but complimentary attributes that, when combined in leadership and decision-making, result in behaviours that are responsible, ethical, and far-sighted. Wise leaders adopt a broader perspective, considering the ethical, emotional, and long-term repercussions of their actions, whereas prudent leaders carefully examine risks and consequences. Because of this synergy, the leadership and decisions that are made are intelligent and ethical.

Chapter 14:

Jesus as the Ultimate Leader: Humility and Sacrifice

It is generally agreed upon that Jesus Christ, the key figure in Christianity, exemplifies the highest level of leadership possible. His life and teachings are characterised by tremendous humility and love that is self-sacrificing, imparting lessons that are ageless for leaders in a variety of fields and fields of endeavour.

Jesus's leadership was built on a firm foundation of humility from the very beginning. In spite of the fact that he was the Son of God, Jesus always acted in a humble manner while interacting with other people. He had a compassionate manner of approaching people, treated them with decency and respect, and freely linked himself with individuals who were considered to be on the margins of society. Because of his humility, Jesus was able to form meaningful connections with people from all walks of life and connect with them on a deeper level.

The willingness of Jesus to serve others is an example of the humility that he had. In order to teach His pupils the value of humility and servant leadership, Jesus washed the disciples' feet, a chore that was traditionally designated for the lowest servant in the household. Jesus demonstrated that genuine leadership is not about exercising control and authority over others, but rather about serving others with compassion and selflessness. He did this by setting an example for others to follow.

Another crucial component of Jesus's leadership is the offering of sacrifice. He gave up His own life voluntarily in order to save the human race. The act of self-sacrifice that Jesus displayed on the crucifixion exemplifies the highest levels of love, compassion, and leadership. This teaches us that true leaders are selfless and willing to make personal sacrifices for the greater welfare of the people they serve, as demonstrated by his sacrifice.

The leadership that Jesus exemplified by His willingness to sacrifice extended to His dedication to forgiveness and reconciliation. Jesus chose to forgive those who harmed him in spite of the fact that he was rejected, betrayed, and executed. His capacity to show mercy and forgiveness even in the face of unimaginable anguish serves as a powerful lesson for those in positions of authority. Leaders may foster an atmosphere of healing, togetherness, and progress within their teams and organisations by adopting forgiveness as a central tenet of their leadership.

In addition to this, Jesus' method of leadership was characterised by a vision that extended beyond the current circumstances. He was sent into the world with the specific task of bringing redemption and reconciliation to people. Jesus was able to clearly explain this vision to His disciples, which spurred them to take action and embrace it. His vision inspired a feeling of purpose and direction in his followers, which motivated them to persevere in the face of adversity and work towards a more lofty objective.

Compassion, empathy, and a genuine care for the health and happiness of others were defining characteristics of Jesus' leadership. He gave healing to the ill, consolation to the heartbroken, and a hand of friendship to those whom society thought worthless. Because of his compassion, Jesus was able to form profound connections with individuals, comprehend their requirements, and offer significant help. A culture of caring, empathy, and support may be fostered inside an organisation by having leaders who model the compassion of Jesus Christ.

The way that Jesus led his followers as an example shakes up traditional conceptions of power and authority. His approach to leadership was characterised by humility, service, sacrifice, forgiveness, and a vision for a world that might be improved. Leaders that exemplify these characteristics have the ability to motivate their followers, cultivate an environment that encourages cooperation, and produce results that are both good and long-lasting.

Key Take Aways:

When incorporated into a person's leadership style, humility and sacrifice are two basic attributes that may inspire and connect a team while also cultivating a culture of selflessness, teamwork, and shared achievement. This can be accomplished by a leader who demonstrates these qualities. The following is an example of how humility and sacrifice may work together to make a leader more effective:

Humbleness:

Being conscious of oneself is the first step towards developing humility. Leaders who are humble have a true grasp of their own strengths and flaws, which enables them to make judgements that are better informed.

Feedback Receptivity Humble leaders are those that are open to receiving feedback and constructive criticism. They make it a point to solicit feedback from other members of the team and then make use of that feedback to develop and advance.

Humility is a quality that frequently goes hand in hand with empathy. Humble leaders are attentive to the wants and emotions of their team members, which helps to develop deeper relationships among the members of the team.

Cooperation: Humble leaders make the importance of cooperation a top priority and respect the contributions made by every member of the team. They cultivate a welcoming atmosphere at work in which everyone is given the opportunity to contribute and is valued for doing so.

The trait of humility is essential to the practise of servant leadership, which emphasises placing a priority on the health and growth of one's team members over one's own personal advancement.

Make a sacrifice:

Putting Others Before Yourself Being a selfless leader means prioritising the requirements of those you lead before your own requirements. Leaders who are prepared to make personal sacrifices for the good of their team are more likely to inspire loyalty and devotion among their followers.

Those who take on the role of sacrificial leaders show their subordinates how to lead by example by demonstrating that they are prepared to put in long hours, make concessions, and commit their time and effort for the benefit of the group as a whole.

Support for the Team Sacrifice might take the form of acts such as contributing direction, mentoring, or resources to assist other members of the team in achieving their goals. Leaders are the ones that go above and above for their teams.

Accountability Is Shared Sacrificial leaders take on a proportionate part of the responsibility for the successes and failures of the team. They accept group accountability rather than assigning blame to individual members of the team.

Long-Term Vision: Leaders that are willing to make sacrifices for the greater benefit of their team or organisation frequently have a long-term vision for their group. They are aware that in order to achieve success in the long run, it may be necessary to make compromises in the near term.

The Complementarity of Self-Sacrifice and Modesty

Improved Morale in the Team When leaders exhibit both humility and sacrifice, it results in improved morale in the team. When leaders are prepared to make sacrifices for the success of their teams, the members of such teams feel respected, supported, and inspired by their leaders.

Trust and Loyalty: Leaders who are humble and willing to make sacrifices for their teams cultivate a high level of trust and loyalty among their followers. The members of the team have faith in the leader's upright character and noble goals.

Culture of Collaboration: The complementary nature of humility and self-sacrifice helps to cultivate a culture of collaboration within a team, one in which members are encouraged to support one another and collaborate with one another to achieve shared objectives.

The ability to change one's leadership style to suit changing conditions requires humility and selflessness on the part of the leader. The act of sacrificing oneself may entail adapting one's tactics or taking on new tasks for the good of the team.

Resilience is exhibited by leaders who are humble and willing to sacrifice themselves in the face of adversity. They are unwavering in their commitment to the health and prosperity of the group, even when things are rough.

The combination of humility and sacrifice in leadership yields an attitude that is unselfish and supportive, which inspires members of the team, establishes trust, and produces a working atmosphere that is collaborative and thriving. Leaders that embody these characteristics demonstrate to followers the importance of placing the requirements of the team ahead of their own, which eventually results in increased productivity and cohesion within the organisation.

Chapter 15:

The Apostles' Unity and Collaboration: Building a Strong Leadership Team

The cooperation and harmony that existed among the apostles in the early Christian community might serve as an instructive example of an effective way to construct a great leadership team. Their combined efforts, common goal, and mutual support provide leaders with significant insights that may be used to the development of unity and collaboration within their own teams.

After the ascension of Jesus, the apostles were tasked with the monumental undertaking of disseminating the message of Christianity and laying the foundation for the early church. Although they came from a variety of places, had different experiences, and had unique personalities, they were able to form a cohesive group because they were working towards the same goal.

Their convergence around a common goal was one of the most important characteristics that contributed to the apostles' ability to work together effectively. They were devoted to preaching the message of love, redemption, and salvation that Jesus taught and felt that his teachings should be followed. The apostles were able to feel a feeling of belonging and camaraderie thanks to this common goal, which served as a uniting force that was able to look past individual distinctions.

Additionally, the apostles were aware of the significance of working together. They collaborated to achieve their goal, combining their respective qualities, abilities, and resources in the process. They were there for one another, took turns shouldering tasks, and made choices as a group. Through working together, they were able to have the most possible influence, make the most of the contributions of members with varying points of view, and triumph over obstacles as a cohesive unit.

The apostles placed a high priority on having honest conversations and paying attention to what others had to say. They communicated with one another in a civil manner, discussed their thoughts and concerns, and looked for common ground on significant issues. They were able to handle disagreements and come to choices collaboratively because they had established a culture of trust and transparency within their team by adopting a communication culture that emphasised openness and transparency.

In addition to this, the apostles modelled the characteristics of humility and servant leadership. They were ready to put their own aspirations and egos to the side in order to put the requirements of the community and the overarching goal first. Because of their modesty, an atmosphere of trust and respect was developed, one in which every member was made to feel appreciated and given permission to offer the particular set of skills and abilities that make them special.

The apostles' ability to work together and maintain their unity was not without its difficulties. They were confronted with arguments and conflicts, but they managed to handle them with grace and a dedication to reconciling with one another. It is a credit to their profound sense of purpose and their dedication to the goal that they all shared that they were able to settle problems and preserve togetherness despite the disparities that existed among them.

From the apostles' ability to work together in harmony and unity, leaders may learn significant lessons. Leaders are able to construct powerful and cohesive teams via the promotion of open communication, encouraging cooperation, and the cultivation of a common vision. They have the ability to cultivate an atmosphere that values the contributions of individuals with varying points of view, encourages constructive resolution of disagreements, and fosters a sense of ownership and dedication to the team's overall goal.

In these last few chapters of this book, we have looked at a variety of leadership principles that may be found in the Bible. Each tale has offered great lessons for leaders who are seeking to become more successful and influential in their jobs, from the wisdom of Solomon to the courage of David, the integrity of Joseph, and the humility of Jesus. These ideas can be found throughout the Bible.

Leaders may inspire their colleagues, develop cooperation, and create a pleasant and empowering work atmosphere all by incorporating these concepts into their approach to leadership. The narratives of these biblical heroes serve as evergreen reminders of the characteristics and principles that drive outstanding leadership, so directing leaders on their own paths of development, education, and metamorphosis as they go through life.

Key Take Aways:

The development of a capable leadership team is critical to the accomplishment of any organization's goals. A leadership team that is cohesive and efficient helps to establish the tone for the entire organisation, encourages innovative thinking, and makes certain that strategic goals are achieved. The following are measures that may be taken to develop a powerful leadership team:

Define the Roles of Leadership and the Expectations Placed on It:

You need to make sure that the duties, responsibilities, and expectations that come along with each leadership position on the team are very clear. This comprises definitions of job responsibilities, important performance metrics, and overall strategy goals.

Choose the Right People to Be on Your Team:

Select leaders who already have the knowledge, experience, and personality traits that are a good cultural fit for their positions. You should look for people whose talents will complement each other's and who can add a variety of perspectives to the team.

Communication and a Sense of Direction:

Encourage communication that is both open and honest among the members of the team. Ensure that all members of the team are in agreement with the organization's mission, vision, and the goals of the strategic strategy.

Establishing trust:

Every successful organisation is built on a solid foundation of trust. Build trust in others by demonstrating honesty, dependability, and responsibility in all you do. Trust-building activities and exercises that emphasise the importance of working together can also be beneficial.

Establish an Environment Favourable to Collaboration:

Encourage a culture of cooperation within your team, one in which members of the group support one another and work together to achieve shared goals. It is important to have regular meetings and sessions for brainstorming.

Foster Creativity and Innovation:

Encourage an atmosphere within the team that values creative problem-solving and innovative approaches to problem-solving. Inspire the people of your team to think creatively and investigate other approaches to resolving problems.

Empower the People, then Delegate:

Give members of the team the authority to make choices within the scope of their assigned responsibilities. It is possible for leaders to concentrate on their primary responsibilities when they delegate authority, which also encourages individual development.

Learning New Things and Improving Yourself Constantly:

Make sure the members of the leadership team have plenty of opportunity to learn new things and improve their existing talents. The value of programmes for training, mentoring, and professional development cannot be overstated.

The Resolution of Conflict:

Create a method for dealing with disagreements and problems that may arise inside the team. Discussions should be encouraged in an open and polite environment so that constructive solutions may be found.

The Establishment of Objectives and the Analysis of Performance:

Establish goals that are both lucid and quantifiable for the individual members of the leadership team. Maintain regular assessments and evaluations of performance in relation to these goals.

The importance of diversity and inclusion:

Promote an inclusive and diverse culture among the members of the leadership team. When members of a team come from a variety of backgrounds, they bring with them a variety of viewpoints and experiences, which can contribute to improved decision-making.

Decision-Making That Is Efficient:

Establish a method for making decisions that is both organised and open to participation from all relevant members of the team. Make sure that the decisions you make are in line with the mission and values of the organisation.

Feedback on a Regular Basis:

It is important to provide members of the team regular feedback. You should encourage children to discuss their thoughts and worries, and you should also be open to accepting criticism from them.

Adjust Yourself to the New:

In the face of change, demonstrate adaptability and flexibility. The ability to adapt one's plans and methods in response to shifting conditions is an essential quality for leaders to possess.

Setting a Good Example:

The members of the leadership team should serve as an example of the behaviours and values they want to see shown by the rest of the organisation. Their deeds serve as the template for how the company's culture should be.

Taking Responsibility:

Make the members of the leadership team responsible for their obligations as well as their performance. Determine the repercussions that will result from falling short of the expectations.

Rejoice in Your Victories:

It is important to acknowledge and rejoice in the successes of the leadership team as well as the organisation. Recognising and appreciating one's achievements contributes to increased motivation and a more upbeat atmosphere at work.

The formation of a capable leadership group is a process that never ends. It demands a commitment to continuously enhancing the efficacy of the team, as well as to promoting cooperation and the development of talent. Organisations that are successful have strong leadership teams that inspire their whole workforce, steer the organisation in the direction of its strategic goals, and are the backbone of the organisation.

Bible References

The Wisdom of Solomon: Leading with Discernment

- Solomon's accession to the throne: 1 Kings 1:39
- The story of the two women claiming to be the mother of the baby: 1 Kings 3:16-28
- Solomon's request for wisdom: 1 Kings 3:5-14
- Solomon's establishment of laws and regulations:
  - 1 Kings 3:15 (mention of his judgments)
  - 1 Kings 4:29-34 (his wisdom and knowledge)
- Solomon's diplomatic alliances and strategic decision-making: 1 Kings 3:1 (his marriage to the daughter of Pharaoh)
- Solomon's reliance on God and seeking divine guidance:
  - 1 Kings 3:3 (Solomon loved the Lord)
  - 1 Kings 3:14 (God's response to Solomon's request for wisdom)

Moses and the Exodus: Visionary Leadership in Times of Crisis

- ✓ Moses' calling and God's plan:
  - ➢ The burning bush and God's call: Exodus 3:1-22
  - ➢ Moses' initial hesitation and self-doubt: Exodus 4:1-17
- ✓ Moses' confronting Pharaoh:
  - ➢ Moses' interactions with Pharaoh and the demand to let the Israelites go: Exodus 5:1-6:13
  - ➢ Pharaoh's refusal and the ten plagues: Exodus 7:14-12:36
- ✓ Parting of the Red Sea and Moses' faith:
  - ➢ The crossing of the Red Sea: Exodus 14:1-31
  - ➢ Moses' trust in God's power and divine intervention: Exodus 14:15-16
- ✓ Adaptability and resilience of Moses:
  - ➢ Moses guiding the Israelites through challenges in the wilderness: Exodus 15:22-27, Exodus 16:1-36, Exodus 17:1-7
  - ➢ Moses promoting unity and providing solutions: Various passages in Exodus
- ✓ Moses as a moral guide and arbitrator of justice:
- ✓ Moses receiving the Ten Commandments: Exodus 20:1-21
- ✓ Moses as an intermediary between God and the people: Various passages in Exodus

David and Goliath: Courage and Strategic Thinking

✓ Introduction to the story of David and Goliath:
  ➢ The story of David and Goliath is primarily found in 1 Samuel 17.
✓ David's courage and faith:
  ➢ David volunteering to face Goliath and his trust in God's providence: 1 Samuel 17:32-37
  ➢ David's courage in the face of Goliath and its effect on the Israelite army: 1 Samuel 17:48-52
✓ David's strategic thinking and use of his sling:
  ➢ David's strategy for defeating Goliath: 1 Samuel 17:40-50
✓ David's leadership and preparation as a shepherd:
  ➢ David's background as a shepherd and his experience defending his sheep: 1 Samuel 17:34-37
  ➢ David's humility and purpose: David's humility and service to King Saul: Various passages in 1 Samuel

Joseph's Journey: Integrity and Resilience in Leadership

✓ Joseph's favouritism, jealousy, and sale into slavery:
  ➢ The story of Joseph's favouritism and his brothers' jealousy: Genesis 37:1-11
  ➢ Joseph being sold into slavery and taken to Egypt: Genesis 37:12-36
✓ Joseph's integrity and resilience as a slave in Potiphar's house:

- ➤ Joseph's honesty and integrity while serving in Potiphar's house: Genesis 39:1-23
- ➤ Joseph's refusal to compromise his values when tempted by Potiphar's wife: Genesis 39:6-20
- ✓ Joseph's imprisonment and interpretation of dreams:
  - ➤ Joseph's imprisonment and continued integrity: Genesis 39:20-23
  - ➤ Joseph interpreting the dreams of fellow prisoners and officials: Genesis 40:1-41:57.
- ✓ Joseph's leadership and foresight during the famine:
  - ➤ Joseph's role in preparing for the famine and providing for the people: Genesis 41:53-57
  - ➤ Joseph's management during the famine: Genesis 41:53-57
- ✓ Reconciliation and forgiveness with his brothers:
  - ➤ Joseph's reconciliation with his brothers and forgiveness: Genesis 45:1-15, Genesis 50:15-21

Nehemiah and Rebuilding the Wall: Mobilizing and Inspiring a Team

- ✓ Nehemiah's call to rebuild the wall of Jerusalem:
  - ➤ Nehemiah's role as the cupbearer to King Artaxerxes and his mission to rebuild the wall: Nehemiah 1:1-11
- ✓ Nehemiah's vision and dedication:
  - ➤ Nehemiah's vision and determination to rebuild the wall: Nehemiah 2:17-18
- ✓ Nehemiah's communication and motivation:

- ➢ Nehemiah addressing the people and explaining the importance of their mission: Nehemiah 2:17-18
- ➢ Nehemiah's empathetic communication and personal connection to the city: Nehemiah 1:4-11
- ✓ Delegation of responsibilities and teamwork:
  - ➢ Nehemiah assigning tasks and responsibilities to different groups of people: Nehemiah 3:1-32
- ✓ Nehemiah's resilience and leadership in the face of challenges:
  - ➢ Opposition and challenges faced by Nehemiah: Nehemiah 4:1-23
  - ➢ Nehemiah's determination and leadership during opposition: Nehemiah 4:14
- ✓ Problem-solving and strategic thinking:
  - ➢ Nehemiah's strategies to defend the workers and ensure their safety: Nehemiah 4:13-23

Deborah and Barak: Collaboration and Empowering Others

- ✓ Deborah's leadership as a judge and prophetess:
  - ➢ Deborah's role as a judge and mediator of disputes: Judges 4:4-5
  - ➢ The oppression of the Israelites by the Canaanites: Judges 4:1-3
- ✓ Deborah's call to Barak and his hesitation:
  - ➢ Deborah's message to Barak from God: Judges 4:6-7
  - ➢ Barak's hesitation and request for Deborah to go with him: Judges 4:8-10

- ✓ Collaboration between Deborah and Barak:
  - ➢ Deborah agreeing to go with Barak and their strategic planning: Judges 4:9, Judges 4:14-16
- ✓ Empowering others and shared leadership:
  - ➢ Deborah's prophecy of victory and giving credit to a woman: Judges 4:9
  - ➢ Deborah's willingness to empower Barak and work collaboratively: Judges 4:9
- ✓ Inclusivity, humility, and open-mindedness:
  - ➢ Deborah's inclusive leadership style and open-mindedness: Judges 4:14

Daniel's Exemplary Character: Leading with Integrity in a Hostile Environment

- ✓ Daniel's unwavering commitment to God and his moral principles:
  - ➢ Daniel's dedication to God while living in Babylon: Daniel 1:8-16
  - ➢ Daniel's faith and trust in God despite facing challenges: Daniel 2:17-23
- ✓ Daniel's response to King Darius's decree and his commitment to prayer:
  - ➢ Daniel's refusal to compromise his religious values in the face of King Darius's decree: Daniel 6:6-10
  - ➢ Daniel's continued prayer to God despite the risk to his life: Daniel 6:11-23
- ✓ Daniel's integrity and Favor with kings:
  - ➢ Daniel's integrity and Favor with King Nebuchadnezzar: Daniel 2:46-49

- ➤ Daniel's honesty and Favor with King Belshazzar: Daniel 5:10-12
- ➤ Daniel's wisdom and leadership abilities in advising kings: Daniel 2:26-28, Daniel 4:27
- ✓ Seeking guidance from God and humility in leadership:
  - ➤ Daniel seeking God's guidance and wisdom in interpreting dreams: Daniel 2:17-18
  - ➤ Daniel's humility and focus on bringing glory to God: Daniel 2:27-28

Ruth's Loyalty and Servant Leadership

- ✓ Ruth's unwavering loyalty to Naomi:
  - ➤ Ruth's declaration of loyalty to Naomi: Ruth 1:16-17
  - ➤ Ruth's commitment to staying with Naomi: Ruth 1:18
- ✓ Ruth's selfless acts of service:
  - ➤ Ruth's willingness to glean in the fields to provide for Naomi: Ruth 2:2-3
  - ➤ Boaz's recognition of Ruth's generous acts and her character: Ruth 2:11-12
- ✓ Boaz's recognition of Ruth's servant leadership:
  - ➤ Boaz's acknowledgment of Ruth's humility and faithfulness: Ruth 2:11-12

Joshua and the Battle of Jericho: Leading with Boldness and Faith

- ✓ God's promise to Joshua and the Israelites:

- ➢ God's command to Joshua and the promise of victory: Joshua 6:2-5
- ✓ Joshua's leadership, courage, and faith:
  - ➢ Joshua's obedience and instructions to march around Jericho: Joshua 6:6-14
  - ➢ The account of the walls of Jericho falling down: Joshua 6:15-21
  - ➢ Joshua's leadership in executing God's strategic plan: Joshua 6:20-21

Esther's Influence: Leadership through Diplomacy and Risk-taking

- ✓ Esther's rise to the position of queen:
  - ➢ Esther's selection as queen: Esther 2:17-18
- ✓ Esther's diplomatic approach:
  - ➢ Esther's strategic planning and inviting the king and Haman to banquets: Esther 5:1-8, Esther 7:1-6
- ✓ Esther's courageous risk-taking:
  - ➢ Esther's willingness to reveal her Jewish heritage for the greater good: Esther 4:12-16, Esther 7:3-4
- ✓ The significance of empathy and speaking up for others:
  - ➢ The theme of Esther's mission to save her people: Esther 4:14
  - ➢ The deliverance and protection of the Jewish people: Esther 8:11-17

Paul's Transformation: From Persecutor to Apostle of the Early Church

- ✓ Paul's encounter on the road to Damascus:
  - ➢ Acts 9:1-19
- ✓ Paul's transformation and new commitment to Christ:
  - ➢ Galatians 1:11-17
  - ➢ 2 Corinthians 5:17
- ✓ Paul's resilience and endurance as an apostle:
  - ➢ 2 Corinthians 11:24-28
  - ➢ 2 Timothy 4:7-8
- ✓ Paul's missionary journeys and leadership role in the early Christian church:
  - ➢ Acts 13-28 (These chapters detail Paul's missionary journeys)
  - ➢ Acts 14:21-28 (Paul and Barnabas returning from their first missionary journey)

Peter's Leadership in the Early Christian Community: Learning from Mistakes

- ✓ Peter's call to be a disciple:
  - ➢ Matthew 4:18-20
  - ➢ Mark 1:16-18
  - ➢ Luke 5:1-11
- ✓ Peter's denial of Jesus:
  - ➢ Matthew 26:69-75
  - ➢ Mark 14:66-72
  - ➢ Luke 22:54-62
  - ➢ John 18:15-18, 25-27

- ✓ Peter's reconciliation with Jesus and commission as a shepherd:
  - ➢ John 21:15-17
- ✓ Peter's leadership in the early Christian community:
  - ➢ Acts 2:14-41 (Peter's sermon on the day of Pentecost)
  - ➢ Acts 10:34-35 (Peter's recognition of God's impartiality)
  - ➢ 1 Peter 5:1-4 (Peter's exhortation to fellow elders)
  - ➢ 2 Peter 1:3-4 (Peter's teachings on godly living and knowledge)

Prudence and Wisdom: Lessons from Proverbs for Effective Leadership

- ✓ Proverbs on Prudence:
  - ➢ Proverbs 8:12: "I, wisdom, dwell together with prudence; I possess knowledge and discretion."
  - ➢ Proverbs 14:15: "The simple believe anything, but the prudent give thought to their steps."
- ✓ Proverbs on Wisdom:
  - ➢ Proverbs 2:6: "For the Lord gives wisdom; from his mouth come knowledge and understanding."
  - ➢ Proverbs 3:13: "Blessed are those who find wisdom, those who gain understanding."
- ✓ Proverbs on Humility:
  - ➢ Proverbs 11:2: "When pride comes, then comes disgrace, but with humility comes wisdom."
  - ➢ Proverbs 15:33: "Wisdom's instruction is to fear the Lord, and humility comes before honor."

- ✓ Proverbs on Communication:
  - ➢ Proverbs 16:23: "The hearts of the wise make their mouths prudent, and their lips promote instruction."
  - ➢ Proverbs 25:11: "A word fitly spoken is like apples of gold in settings of silver."
- ✓ Proverbs on Honesty and Morality:
  - ➢ Proverbs 11:3: "The integrity of the upright guides them, but the unfaithful are destroyed by their duplicity."
  - ➢ Proverbs 28:6: "Better the poor whose walk is blameless than the rich whose ways are perverse."

Jesus as the Ultimate Leader: Humility and Sacrifice

- ✓ **Humility:**
  - ➢ Philippians 2:5-8: "In your relationships with one another, have the same mindset as Christ Jesus: Who, being in very nature God, did not consider equality with God something to be used to his own advantage; rather, he made himself nothing by taking the very nature of a servant, being made in human likeness. And being found in appearance as a man, he humbled himself by becoming obedient to death— even death on a cross!"
- ✓ **Service and Sacrifice:**
  - ➢ Mark 10:45: "For even the Son of Man did not come to be served, but to serve, and to give his life as a ransom for many."

- John 13:14-15: "Now that I, your Lord and Teacher, have washed your feet, you also should wash one another's feet. I have set you an example that you should do as I have done for you."

✓ **Forgiveness:**
- Luke 23:34: "Jesus said, 'Father, forgive them, for they do not know what they are doing.'"
- Matthew 18:21-22: "Then Peter came to Jesus and asked, 'Lord, how many times shall I forgive my brother or sister who sins against me? Up to seven times?' Jesus answered, 'I tell you, not seven times, but seventy-seven times.'"

✓ **Vision:**
- Matthew 28:19-20: "Therefore go and make disciples of all nations, baptizing them in the name of the Father and of the Son and of the Holy Spirit, and teaching them to obey everything I have commanded you. And surely I am with you always, to the very end of the age."

✓ **Compassion and Empathy:**
- Matthew 14:14: "When Jesus landed and saw a large crowd, he had compassion on them and healed their sick."
- Hebrews 4:15: "For we do not have a high priest who is unable to empathize with our weaknesses, but we have one who has been tempted in every way, just as we are—yet he did not sin."

The Apostles' Unity and Collaboration: Building a Strong Leadership Team

✓ **Common Goal and Unity:**
  ➢ Acts 4:32: "All the believers were one in heart and mind. No one claimed that any of their possessions was their own, but they shared everything they had."

✓ **Collaboration and Working Together:**
  ➢ Acts 6:2-4: "So the Twelve gathered all the disciples together and said, 'It would not be right for us to neglect the ministry of the word of God to wait on tables. Brothers and sisters, choose seven men from among you who are known to be full of the Spirit and wisdom. We will turn this responsibility over to them and will give our attention to prayer and the ministry of the word.'"

✓ **Honest Communication and Resolution:**
  ➢ Acts 15:6-7: "The apostles and elders met to consider this question. After much discussion, Peter got up and addressed them: 'Brothers, you know that some time ago God made a choice among you that the Gentiles might hear from my lips the message of the gospel and believe.'"

✓ **Humility and Servant Leadership:**
  ➢ Mark 9:35: "Sitting down, Jesus called the Twelve and said, 'Anyone who wants to be first must be the very last, and the servant of all.'"
  ➢ Acts 20:19: "I served the Lord with great humility and with tears and in the midst of severe testing by the plots of my Jewish opponents."

- ✓ **Reconciliation and Handling Conflicts:**
  - ➢ Matthew 18:15: "If your brother or sister sins, go and point out their fault, just between the two of you. If they listen to you, you have won them over."
  - ➢ 1 Corinthians 1:10: "I appeal to you, brothers and sisters, in the name of our Lord Jesus Christ, that all of you agree with one another in what you say and that there be no divisions among you, but that you be perfectly united in mind and thought."

End Note:

Throughout the entirety of this book, "**Leadership Lessons from the Bible: Insights for Becoming an Effective Leader**," we have examined the narratives of a variety of biblical people and the leadership skills that they possessed that served as an example for us. Each chapter provides leaders in a variety of settings with useful insights and lessons, ranging from the understanding of Solomon to the cohesion of the apostles.

These chapters have shed light on fundamental leadership abilities such as discernment, visionary thinking, integrity, resilience, cooperation, empowerment, diplomacy, risk-taking, and humility. These talents are needed for successful leaders. By establishing a connection between these lessons and the stories and lessons taught in the Bible, the incorporation of Bible passages has helped to further expand our knowledge.

The lives and leadership experiences of these biblical heroes have provided us with insights into timeless principles and practical advice that may be applied to contemporary management dilemmas. The decisions that these biblical leaders made, how they navigated hostile situations, how they managed varied teams, and how they led in times of crisis are all areas in which these leaders' examples give invaluable direction and inspiration.

It is my sincere desire that this book has been able to serve as a resource and a guide for those who aspire to be leaders as well as those who are already in leadership positions, providing them with ageless concepts and insights that may help their development and efficiency. These teachings on leadership from the Bible should motivate those in positions of authority to lead with honesty and humility, as well as a dedication to serving the needs of those around them so that they might have a beneficial effect on the communities in which they are involved.

www.ingramcontent.com/pod-product-compliance
Lightning Source LLC
LaVergne TN
LVHW061618070526
838199LV00078B/7336